CONTENTS

NOTE

In order to simplify the use of this book, all names, locations and geographic designations are as provided in *The Times World Atlas*, or other traditionally accepted major sources of reference, as of the time of the events described. Arabic names are romanised and transcripted rather than transliterated. For example, the definite article 'al-' before words starting with 'sun letters' is given as pronounced instead of simply as 'al-' (which is the usual practice for non-Arabic speakers in most English-language literature and media).

Helion & Company Limited
26 Willow Road, Solihull, West Midlands, B91 1UE, England
Tel. 0121 705 3393
Fax 0121 711 4075
Email: info@helion.co.uk   Website: www.helion.co.uk   Twitter: @helionbooks   Visit our blog http://blog.helion.co.uk/

Published by Helion & Company 2017
Designed and typeset by Farr out Publications, Wokingham, Berkshire
Cover designed by Paul Hewitt, Battlefield Design (www.battlefield-design.co.uk)
Printed by Henry Ling Ltd, Dorchester, Dorset

Text © David Nicolle, Tom Cooper and Air Vice Marshal Gabr Ali Gabr (ret.) 2017
Photographs © as individually credited
Colour profiles © Tom Cooper 2016

ISBN 978-1-911096-61-0

British Library Cataloguing-in-Publication Data.
A catalogue record for this book is available from the British Library.

For details of other military history titles published by Helion & Company Limited contact the above address, or visit our website: http://www.helion.co.uk. We always welcome receiving book proposals from prospective authors.

ACKNOWLEDGMENTS

The authors would like to thank the many participants mentioned in this book, who kindly shared often intriguing personal stories or eyewitness accounts. Foremost are the officers and pilots of the Egyptian Air Force (and former Royal Egyptian Air Force, EAF/ REAF), who kindly shared recollections and documentation with us. Those we feel free to mention include Air Marshal Tahir Zaki (EAF), Air Marshal Mustafa Shalabi el-Hinnawy (EAF), Air Marshal Ala Barakat (EAF ret.), Air Marshal Farouq el-Ghazzawi (EAF ret.), Air Vice-Marshal Abd al-Moneim Mikaati (EAF ret.), Air Vice-Marshal Sa'ad ad-Din Sherif (EAF), Major-General Mohammad Okasha (EAF ret.), Major-General Mamdouh Taliba (EAF ret.), Air Commodore Mustafa Hafez (EAF), Air Commodore Fuad Kamal (EAF ret.), Air Commodore Abdel Moneim el-Tawil (EAF ret.), Air Commodore Ibrahim Gazerine (EAF ret.), Wing Commander Kamal Zaki (EAF ret.), Wing Commander Talaat Louca (EAF ret.), Wing Commander Usama Sidqi (EAF ret.) and Squadron Leader Wagdi Hafez (EAF ret.).

We would like to express our special thanks to Martin Smisek from the Czech Republic for personally working through the Czech National Archive for many years, and also to thank Nour Bardai, Dr Abdallah Emran and Sherif Sharmi from Egypt, and Albert Grandolini from France for running additional interviews and faithfully providing plenty of precious bits and pieces of information over the years. We wish to thank Ass'aad Dib in Lebanon for his translations of Ali Muhammad Labib's history of the Egyptian Air Force, and Lon Nordeen in the USA for permission to use some of his research, including interviews with a number of Egyptian participants of this war. Our thanks go to Mr Tarek el-Shennawy, Mrs Leila, the late Mrs Khouda and the late Mrs Mona Tewfik for permission to use their family archives. Last, but not least, our thanks go to Farzin Nadimi for his research in the archives of the Air Ministry in Great Britain, to Christof Hahn for help with further research in general and to Hicham Honeini from Lebanon for his patience and kind help with translations of various publications and documentation from Arabic.

ABBREVIATIONS

AAA	anti-aircraft artillery
AB	air base
AdA	Armée de l'Air (French Air Force)
BOAC	British Overseas Airways Corporation
CIA	Central Intelligence Agency (USA)
CO	commanding officer
DMZ	de-militarised zone
EAF	Egyptian Air Force (official designation from 1952–1958)
ELINT	electronic intelligence
FCU	Fighter Conversion Unit
FTU	Fighter Training Unit
IAP	international airport
IDF	Israeli Defence Force
IDF/AF	Israeli Defence Force/Air Force
Il	Ilyushin (the design bureau led by Sergey Vladimirovich Ilyushin, also known as OKB-39)
KIA	killed in action
METO	Middle Eastern Treaty Organisation
MiG	Mikoyan i Gurevich (the design bureau led by Artyom Ivanovich Mikoyan and Mikhail Iosifovich Gurevich, also known as OKB-155 or MMZ 'Zenit')
MOD	Ministry of Defence
NATO	North Atlantic Treaty Organisation
NEACC	Near East Arms Coordinating Committee
OCU	Operational Conversion Unit
OTU	Operational Training Unit
PAO	Pilot Attack Officer
PBG	Palestinian Border Guard
POW	prisoner of war
RAF	Royal Air Force (United Kingdom)
REAF	Royal Egyptian Air Force
rpm	rounds per minute
SyAAF	Syrian Arab Air Force
UN	United Nations
UNRWA	United Nations Relief and Works Agency for Palestine Refugees in the Near East
UNSC	United Nations Security Council
USSR	Union of Soviet Socialist Republics (also Soviet Union)

1

GEO-POLITICAL BACKGROUNDS

The short but bitter 'Suez Crisis of 1956' is a relatively well-known affair, about which dozens of books and thousands of articles have been published. Most histories published in the West were written during the Cold War. As usual during those times, every political move by either side was directed, or at any rate judged to be directed by its opponents, towards influencing ideologically uncommitted nations. Those gleeful neutrals who dared accept the trade and aid showered upon them became either 'dupes of Communism' or 'lackeys of Imperialism', according to which side's 'bribes' they pocketed or to what kind of threats they were subjected. Egypt, therefore, ended on the list of 'allies', or at least 'customers', of the former Union of Soviet Socialist Republics (USSR, or Soviet Union). This has distorted many accounts, especially where the motivation and reasoning of the Egyptians themselves were concerned. Indeed, with a handful of exceptions, accounts rarely depict the Egyptian version of events. Sometimes this is intentional, other times not, but the result is always the same: plenty of important parts of the story remain unknown and the usual versions are therefore greatly distorted.

The following account is based on Egyptian documentation about this conflict collected over decades by late Air Vice Marshal Gabr Ali Gabr (EAF); on interviews with a number of Egyptian participants (see acknowledgments and endnotes); and further documentation declassified over time by various national archives. Its centrepiece is a detailed operational history of the EAF during the Suez War, and insights into the doctrine, strategy, organisation, training, motivation and competence of this service. Many foreign accounts grossly exaggerate or understate many of the factors in question. Above all, the motivation and competence of Egyptian airmen have been questioned. In fact, the EAF is frequently described as barely taking part in the conflict against the Israeli invaders, losing the campaign and then entirely disappearing from the skies and being completely destroyed by the British and French.

In reality, the EAF fought the Israeli invaders with much more gusto than it fought the British and French, as this story will show, but it also avoided complete destruction. Furthermore, this account will show that while the Egyptians were overawed by those who until very recently had been their teachers, and suffered from an understandable feeling of inferiority when facing the powerful air forces of both Britain and France, no such lack of confidence and professionalism burdened the EAF when it took on Israeli forces.

Our hope is that the result is going to further more critical studies of this war, and also improve understanding of the Arab-Israeli conflict in general.

THE TRIPARTITE DECLARATION

Histories of the Suez War tend to start with the Egyptian Revolution of 1952, then describe the revolution's impact upon relations between the new government in Cairo, Israel and various Western powers. Nearly all published Western accounts maintain that it was the decision by Egyptian President Gamal Abdel Nasser to order arms from the Soviet Union, and then to nationalise the Suez Canal, that was the primary reasons for the outbreak of the Suez Crisis. Few accounts go as far as to point out that this conflict marked the occasion when two worlds came into collision, when two imperialist Western powers attempted, unsuccessfully, to reassert both their

authority and prestige in the face of Arab nationalism.

Israeli narratives usually have a sort of pre-emptive attack as their centrepiece. Accordingly, after defeat in the First Arab-Israeli War of 1947-1949 (known as the Palestine War in Egypt), Arab governments were regarded as always seeking an opportunity to launch another war, while sponsoring terrorist activities against Israel, and blocking strategically important waterways to all shipping bound for Israel. The Egyptian decision to acquire arms from the USSR then supposedly resulted in an arms race, while the nationalisation of the Suez Canal left Israel with no choice but to strike first.

From the Egyptian point of view, the background was far simpler and primarily related to the issue of Egypt having long been a victim of Western imperialism, then being the victim of an unprovoked tripartite aggression aimed at removing the government in Cairo which sought to keep the country out of the Cold War, and finally as being the victim of another Israeli land grab.

From the standpoint of academic historians, it all began back in 1882, when Great Britain occupied Egypt – supposedly out of concern for the security of the Suez Canal, the 'lifeline of the Empire'. This period of British control is often described as 'mutually beneficial, if distasteful to Egyptians because of British paternalism and racial disdain'.[1] In 1922, nominal independence was bestowed upon Egypt, but Britain remained in effective control of the country and would use it as the base of operations against the Axis in the Western Desert and Mediterranean between 1940 and 1943. The defeat of the Germans and Italians was seen as removing any threat to Egypt – but only from the British point of view. In contrast, the establishment of the state of Israel subsequently caused a major readjustment of Egyptian security interests: all of a sudden, these were wholly at odds with British concerns. Even though Britain agreed to evacuate Egypt in 1946, her forces remained deployed in the Canal Zone, where they remained an affront to Egyptian demands for self-determination and the wider issue of Arab nationalism.

When Egypt and Israel signed their armistice agreement and ended the Palestine War, on 24 February 1949, the Western powers attempted to return to 'business as usual', and to stabilise the situation with the Tripartite Declaration. Made by Great Britain, the United States and France on 25 May 1950, this guaranteed the territorial status quo as determined by the Arab-Israeli armistice agreements, outlined the parties' commitment to peace and stability in the area and their opposition to the use or threat of force. Foremost, the Tripartite Declaration reiterated the three great powers' opposition to the emergence of an arms race between the Arab states and Israel. While acknowledging that both sides needed to maintain a certain level of armed forces for the purposes of legitimate self-defence, the three powers agreed to consider all applications for arms or war materials by the countries of the Middle East in the light of these principles.[2]

To strengthen the Tripartite Declaration as a proper instrument of ensuring neutrality in the Arab-Israeli feud of the West in general, and of the USA in particular, the parties set up the Near East Arms Coordinating Committee (NEACC) in June 1952. This body coordinated arms sales to all parties in the conflict. For at least two years, the NEACC functioned reasonably well. Then affairs began to spiral out of control.

UPHEAVALS AND UNREST

In the early 1950s, Great Britain was considered the most powerful nation in the Islamic world. This was because millions of Moslems still lived within its empire, or within its spheres of influence, even

British troops leaving Haifa in June 1948: their withdrawal from Palestine marked the beginning of the end of British hegemony over the Middle East. (Mark Lepko Collection)

Palestinians expelled by Israeli troops to Beach Camp in Gaza boarding boats for Lebanon and Egypt in 1949. The presence of hundreds of thousands of traumatised Palestinian refugees, and defeat during the Palestine War of 1947–1949, had destabilising effects on most Arab countries. (Hrant Nakashian/UNRWA Archives)

Haghanah combatants expelling Palestinians from Haifa on 12 May 1948. (Mark Lepko Collection)

after the Indian subcontinent was granted independence. Second to Britain was France, with its possessions throughout northern and western Africa, and influence in the Middle East, particularly in Lebanon. However, in a matter of just a few years, these positions were shattered beyond repair.

The Palestine War not only failed to unify the Arab world, but led to upheavals in several countries. Such disruptions were often fermented by a new, young and disillusioned generation, which had been nurtured on what was considered the injustice of Zionist dispossession of Arab people and seizure of Arab land with the assistance of Western powers. The humiliating defeat at the hands of Israel first provoked a series of military coups and counter-coups in Syria, which resulted in the rule of Colonel Adib Shishakly between 1950 and 1954. For a while, some Syrian officers played with the thought of realising earlier ideas of joining a union with Iraq, Jordan or Lebanon – especially after Lebanese President Camille Chamoun made corresponding overtures in 1953 – but they abandoned this idea as soon as they realised they would not have senior positions in any resulting authorities. While there is no doubt that the emerging Arab nationalism of the early 1950s found a common focal point in the hatred of Israel, there is equally little doubt that it also disliked what it saw as the reactionary influence of the old dynasties – all of which were linked to Great Britain and France. On 22 November 1952, what began as a demonstration by

schoolchildren in Baghdad, capital of Iraq, developed into arson and riots that forced the government of Premier Nuri as-Said – an old friend of Thomas E. Lawrence ('Lawrence of Arabia') – to impose martial law and deploy troops on the streets. Nominally ruled by King Faysall II, the country took two years to stabilise, and then only after as-Said embarked upon a programme of social improvement, starting in 1954.

In Jordan, Arab refugees from Palestine made up at least a third of the population: although given Jordanian citizenship, they remained a discontented element. One of their number assassinated King Abdullah on 20 July 1951 in the al-Aqsa mosque in Jerusalem. The throne first passed to the older son, and then, in 1952, to the British-educated King Hussein, who was only 17 years of age. Both Egypt and Syria were critical of Hussein's British connections, and eventually encouraged the youthful sovereign to dismiss his British commander of the Jordanian military in 1956. Therefore, what happened in Egypt in 1952 was only one part of an entire mosaic of dramatic developments within the Arab world. But compared with these other contemporary events, the Egyptian Revolution was the one with the furthest-reaching consequences.

BLACK SATURDAY

With the onset of the Cold War, the concerns of British government ministers and military officials extended from securing the Suez Canal Zone to defence of the Middle East as a whole. Crucial for British relations with Egypt was the Anglo-Egyptian treaty of 1936, which allowed Great Britain the right of military intervention against all foreign and domestic threats. Negotiations had been underway since 1946, when British forces withdrew from other parts of Egypt and concentrated within the so-called Suez Canal Zone. However, these negotiations foundered over Cairo's insistence on the unity of Sudan with Egypt under the Egyptian Crown. After the Palestine War, and in the wake of the formation of the North Atlantic Treaty Organisation (NATO), Britain's responsibility for the defence of the Middle East and the Suez Canal Zone in particular remained. Feeling overburdened by all of its commitments, and after unsuccessful attempts to obtain support from Commonwealth countries in Middle East defence, London turned to Cairo for assistance – only to find the Egyptians preoccupied with Israel rather than with the USSR. Indeed, the government of King Farouq was determined to rid Egyptian soil of British troops entirely, irrespective of the

A formation of training aircraft of the Royal Egyptian Air Force participating in a parade staged for the marriage of King Farouq and Queen Farida on 20 January 1938. (Mark Lepko Collection)

Egyptian policemen escorted away from the police station at el-Hamada by British troops, on 16 January 1952. (Mark Lepko Collection)

King Farouq of Egypt in the early 1950s. (Mark Lepko Collection)

consequences for Middle East security.[3]

Unsurprisingly, relations between Egypt and Britain worsened through 1951. Food supplies to British bases in the Suez Canal Zone were cut off and Egyptian civilian labour withdrawn. Guerrilla attacks were carried out by a variety of groups, mainly the Moslem Brotherhood, which preached a fundamentalist creed of Islamic revivalism, but also by communists. On 16 October 1951, the Egyptian parliament, in a unanimous vote, abrogated the 1936 Anglo-Egyptian treaty, prompting London to deploy reinforcements to the Suez Canal Zone. On 25 January 1952, British troops attempted to disarm the auxiliary police force in Ismailia. When the Egyptians resisted, a fierce fire-fight erupted. This took the British officers by surprise; at least 41 stubbornly defending Egyptians were killed, and double that number wounded.[4] This perceived 'massacre' precipitated riots on 26 January 1952 – known as 'Black Saturday' – in the course of which the Moslem Brotherhood, socialists and students, sometimes assisted by Egyptian police angered over the sacrifice of their compatriots in Ismailia, attacked the European quarter of Cairo with cries of 'Allah-u-akbar' and 'We want arms to fight for the Canal'. Symbols of British power in Egypt such as Shepheard's Hotel, travel firm Thomas Cook or offices of the British Overseas Airways Corporation (BOAC), were trashed, together with 400 other buildings, and 11 British nationals were murdered.[5] British retaliation was severe and included the burning down of at least one Egyptian village. By the time order was restored by the firm action of the Egyptian Army, at least 17 civilians and 50 Egyptian police officers had perished, and in excess of £4 million

Members of the RCC after taking power in Cairo. Sitting, from left to right, are Abd el-Latif Boghdadi, Gamal Abdel Nasser, Muhammad Naguib, Abdel Hakim Amer, Gamal Salem and Anwat el-Sadat. (Mark Lepko Collection)

A US-made M4 Sherman tank with Egyptian troops involved in the coup, in front of the Abdin Palace in Cairo, on 26 July 1952. (Mark Lepko Collection)

worth of damage had been caused to British-owned property in Cairo alone.[6]

EGYPTIAN REVOLUTION

Concerned about a possible conflagration, King Farouq ordered his government to improve Anglo-Egyptian relations, but it was too late. On 23 July 1952, Farouq was overthrown in a military coup led by a group of Egyptian military known as the Free Officers Movement; an event which became known as the 'Egyptian Revolution'.

Originally established during the Second World War, and having established cells in all branches of the Egyptian military, the Free Officers now exiled the king and vested all powers in a nine-member Revolution Command Council (RCC), effectively presided over by the strongman of this movement, Lieutenant-Colonel Gamal Abdel Nasser.

Primarily motivated by nationalism, the officers in question had big hopes and great plans. Foremost of these was for the RCC never to install itself in power but to re-establish a parliamentary democracy. Because Nasser did not believe that a low-ranking officer like himself would be accepted by the Egyptian people, and in order to keep the armed forces firmly behind a coup by relatively junior officers, the RCC asked another of the Free Officers Movement's senior members, General Mohammed Naguib Yousef Qotb Elkashlan – one of Egypt's few heroes from the Palestine War of 1948-1949 and a popular figure amongst the public – to assume leadership. When the RCC officially declared Egypt to be a republic on 26 July 1952, Naguib was sworn in as its first President, Prime Minister and Chairman of the RCC, which itself presided over a government largely consisting of army officers. Nasser was appointed Deputy Prime Minister and Minister of the Interior.

THE MARCH CRISIS

A power-struggle between Naguib and other members of the RCC – especially Nasser – developed as early as the summer of 1952.

This was primarily related to the issue of how the revolution's goals would be implemented. Naguib wanted to phase out the political influence of the military and return the country to civilian rule. Impatient and eager to reach their goals, Nasser and other members of the RCC were concerned about the influence of the nationalist liberal Wafd Party, the Moslem Brotherhood, Egyptian communists and various other movements. Therefore, in January 1953, they dissolved and banned all political parties, and declared a three-year transitional period during which the RCC would rule. The Moslem Brotherhood reacted with a campaign of civil tumult and a struggle for popular support. By January 1954, the crisis reached a point at which the RCC felt forced to outlaw the fundamentalist organisation. As street riots spread, Nasser began accusing Naguib of supporting the religious movement and of harbouring dictatorial ambitions, while at the same time launching a campaign to present a favourable image of himself to the Egyptian public. A political struggle between Naguib and Nasser developed that was to last two months. Known as the 'March Crisis', it ended with Naguib retaining the position of president, but losing whatever real authority or political relevancy he once held.[7]

NASSER'S CLIMB TO POWER AND BRITISH WITHDRAWAL

Nasser next published his book, *The Philosophy of the Revolution*. One of several available versions was translated into English and was republished in the USA. Amongst other things, it contained a claim that Egypt lay at the coincidence of three circles: the Arab circle, the African circle and the Islamic circle. Egypt's wealth, size, population, religion and intellectual qualities made it the obvious leader of the Arab world. The emerging Black African nations, struggling for their own independence, would also look to Egypt, which formed the link between Africa and the outside world. Cairo, with its ancient Azhar University, was similarly a major focal point in the Muslim world.[8] Following these principles, and keen to play the leading role but also wishing to improve his standing amongst

Naguib (centre right, with cap) and members of the RCC in 1952, including Nasser (centre), Amer (standing, centre) and Boghdadi (sitting in the background). Within weeks of establishing themselves in power, significant rifts developed between Nasser's supporters and Naguib. (Mark Lepko Collection)

De Havilland Vampire FB.Mk 9s of No. 213 Squadron, RAF, over Egypt in 1952. This unit was based at Deversoir in the Suez Canal Zone at the time, while some 80,000 British troops were stationed in the Canal Zone as a whole. (Mark Lepko Collection)

the population, Nasser initiated serious negotiations concerning the future of Anglo-Egyptian relations and the British garrison of some 80,000 men deployed primarily in the Suez Canal Zone.[9]

The first part of this process was concluded in 1953, with an agreement to terminate British rule in the Sudan in return for Egypt abandoning its claims to suzerainty over the entire Nile Valley. In July 1954, a second agreement was reached. This acknowledged that the Suez Canal was an integral part of Egypt and stipulated a phased evacuation of British troops from bases in the Suez Canal Zone, to be completed within 20 months. Britain nevertheless retained the right to maintain the vacated bases in operational condition, plus some stocks of ammunition and spares, manned by about 1,200 civilian technicians. Futhermore, the British could return in the case of an attack by a foreign power – but notably excluding Israel.[10]

Signed by both sides, three months later this success prompted an emboldened Nasser to deliver a public speech in Alexandria on 26 October. This moment was seized upon by the Moslem Brotherhood, which sent one of its members, Mohammed Abdel Latif, to assassinate the Egyptian strongman. Although getting within 25ft of Nasser and then firing eight shots, Latif nevertheless missed his target. As panic broke out, Nasser maintained his poise and delivered a speech that electrified the audience. The assassination attempt thus not only backfired, but played straight into Nasser's hands. Upon returning to Cairo, he orchestrated one of the largest political crackdowns in the modern history of Egypt, which included the arrest of thousands of members of various opposition groups, while also dismissing 140 officers loyal to General Naguib. Furthermore, Nasser imposed control over the country's media and launched a public relations campaign that promoted his version of nationalism while denigrating his political opponents. Finally, Nasser forced Naguib to resign and had him put under house arrest in a suburban Cairo villa. In January 1955, the RCC appointed Gamal Abdel Nasser as its president – and thus President of Egypt – 'pending national elections'.[11]

AMERICAN MISUNDERSTANDINGS

The 'Arab renaissance' of the early 1950s, its political, cultural and economic manifestations, were not really understood by the leaders of Western powers. Most of them tended to think of 'Arabs' as 'bedouin', and Egyptians as 'something else'. More importantly, they viewed related developments through the prism of the Cold War and interpreted many Arab-related affairs as Soviet intrusions within Western spheres of interest. On the other side, Arab statesmen were especially angered by the British refusal to treat them as equals. Nowhere was this more obvious than in relations between the USA, Great Britain and Egypt in the early 1950s.

The Americans introduced themselves as a new superpower in the Middle East immediately before and during the Palestine War of 1948, when the USA had been a staunch supporter of Israel. Although the administration of President Harry S. Truman subsequently attempted to treat the Arabs and Israel more even-handedly, and was instrumental in the issue of the Tripartite Declaration, all subsequent American actions were viewed with deep suspicion by leading politicians in Cairo and Damascus. Uncertain whom to befriend, the USA relied on Britain and France, despite knowing that British and French influence was resented by most local peoples in the region. Furthermore, believing that fear of the Soviet Union had helped end historic Franco-German enmity, the Americans assumed that anti-Communism would similarly end the Arab-Israeli dispute.[12] Unsurprisingly, most Arab statesmen interpreted things very differently.

This remained the case after President Dwight D. Eisenhower replaced Truman in the White House in January 1953. Washington had maintained ties with Nasser via the Central Intelligence Agency (CIA), and actually regarded Nasser as a 'CIA asset'.[13] Similarly, consistently positive reporting about Nasser by the US ambassador to Cairo, Jefferson Caffery, changed very little in relations between the two nations.[14] Washington remained preoccupied with a possible Soviet penetration of the Middle East and with the idea of creating a defensive alliance similar to NATO, aimed at keeping the USSR out of the region. Unsurprisingly, when John Foster Dulles, Eisenhower's Secretary of State, toured the Middle East in May 1953, he concluded that Arab states were in reality more concerned about Zionism than about the Communists. Nasser, for example, stressed that he did not share US fears of the USSR, but instead expressed his wish to end British influence, not only in Egypt but throughout the Middle East.[15] In the conclusion of his resulting report, Dulles stated that the Egyptians were not interested in joining any Western-dominated alliances, and recommended that US policy towards Egypt worked towards a peace with Israel and a settlement of the Anglo-Egyptian dispute over the Suez Canal. Only then, he concluded, would adhesion to a US-sponsored security pact become possible.[16]

During the course of the next round of US-Egyptian negotiations, in October 1954, and despite the first news of French sale of arms to Israel, Nasser became one of the few heads of state to refuse US military aid, which had been offered by the Eisenhower

The foreign policy of US President Dwight D. Eisenhower was dominated by the Cold War and a determination to prevent the spread of communism. This found little understanding among most Arab statesmen. (Dwight D. Eisenhower Library)

administration. Instead, Egyptian Foreign Minister Fawzy informed Caffery that his country would prefer economic rather than military aid.[17]

FRANCE: THE LAST BASTION

The Anglo-Egyptian withdrawal from the Suez Zone was widely perceived in Britain as the biggest retreat from empire since the division of the Indian subcontinent. Unsurprisingly, it left a particularly bitter taste amongst some circles in London. In combination with the publication of the *The Philosophy of the Revolution*, Nasser's well-known hatred of British imperialism and his claim to be a pan-Arabic leader, it prompted major British political leaders to develop strong antipathies towards Nasser.[18]

The Egyptian strongman then added insult to injury by launching an anti-Imperialist propaganda campaign via the *Sawt al-Arab* (Voice of the Arabs) radio station. Established in 1953 and based in Cairo, it transmitted from an installation outside the city, using many shortwave frequencies across the Middle East, Europe, Africa and even North America. The Voice of the Arabs promoted Nasser's messages of pan-Arabism, Arab unity, rejection of Western imperialism and support for revolutionary fervour. Achieving unmatched popularity, in mid-1954 this radio station expanded its operation by broadcasting in Swahilli in support of the Mau Mau insurgency and inciting black-African British subjects in East Africa into rebellion.[19]

The Philosophy of the Revolution created even more negative feelings in France. Ten years after the end of the Second World War, the French had little with which to console themselves. Their country went through as many as 22 different governments during this period and was widely considered as ungovernable. Liberated from Nazi Germany by the USA and Great Britain, manoeuvred by the British out of Syria and Lebanon, the French suffered disastrous defeat at Dien Bien Phu and were forced to accept the independence of Indochina. It was thus hardly surprising that some French politicians, most notably Prime Minister Guy Mollet, a socialist in sympathy with Israeli socialism, began regarding Nasser's *The Philosophy of the Revolution* as a revised edition of Adolf Hitler's *Mein Kampf*. In reality, of course, this was about as accurate as dubbing the *Sun* newspaper as equivalent to *The Wall Street Journal*. Indeed, members of the French Ministry of Defence (MOD) often drew an analogy between Nasser and Hitler.[20]

Reaction within the French military was even more extreme. Having only just suffered the ignominy of defeat in Indochina, the French Army was determined to win its next war at any price, especially officers who had experienced Viet Minh prison camps and felt a deep need to analyse the reasons for that catastrophe and not to let it happen again. This resulted in various studies and a theory on how best to counter future insurgents. Becoming known as *guerre révolutionnaire*, this was a somewhat restricted view of how to counter native revolutions, almost entirely based upon the strategy propounded by Mao Tse-tung and Ho Chi Minh. Of course, this bore no relation to what they were to face next.[21]

Within a short period, the French found themselves confronted with demands for independence from the three Maghreb states of Morocco, Algeria and Tunisia. In 1955, Paris was left with no alternative but to acknowledge the independence of Morocco, with Tunisia following only a year later.[22] However, the French community in Algeria blocked the application of even an elected assembly, let alone acknowledging the rights of the local indigenous population. This in turn provoked an armed rebellion, which the French military perceived as 'another Communist uprising'.[23]

'Les Paras' were the proud elite of the French military: crack troops led by aggressive and courageous officers, renowned as soldiers from whom impossible efforts were demanded and who were often sent into action to retrieve losing battles. After the catastrophe in Indochina, their commanders were determined to win their next war at any price. (Albert Grandolini Collection)

While the Communist Party of Algeria did exist, it was neither strong nor popular amongst the Algerians. Nevertheless, French military theoreticians remained insistent upon regarding their armed struggle against Algerian nationalists as a last ditch stand against communism. Because of this, they concluded that it was the job of their military – perceived as the only true bastion of the West – to contain and destroy the insurgency, while any negotiations with Algerian nationalists or their supporters was understood as a sign of weakness.

As a party openly supporting the Algerian insurgency – permitting it to establish its headquarters in Cairo – and then being interpreted as a threat similar to that of Nazi Germany in the 1930s, Nasser's government became akin to France's arch enemy.

BLOCKADE OF THE GULF OF AQABA

The situation for Israel in the early 1950s was no better than that of any Arab state. While Jewish refugees from Europe and Jewish money from around the world poured into the country, Israel actually had no national economy and was thus unsustainable. Its two main products were citrus fruits and chemicals extracted from the Dead Sea, but revenues from these exports provided for only 18-25 percent of the national budget. The reminder was made up of numerous foreign loans, charitable contributions from American and European Jews – which were falling at a steady rate – and direct grants-in-aid advanced by the US government.[24]

Although accepting the armistice with Israel, the Arabs refused to recognise her legal existence and now resorted to economic warfare. A complete blockade of all outside relations was consolidated by the closing of the Suez Canal and the existing pipelines connecting oilfields in Iraq via Jordan with Haifa, leaving Israel reliant on oil imported by tankers. In 1949, Israelis attempted to use the port of Eilat in the Gulf of Aqaba, but Egypt deployed artillery units at Sharm el-Sheikh and Ras Nasrani, while Saudi Arabia agreed not to pursue its claim to the Egyptian-held islands of Tiran and Sanafir. Once these were occupied by Egyptian troops in December 1950, the Gulf of Aqaba was closed to Israeli shipping. While causing no direct damage to Israel, these moves restricted sea communications between Israel and the Zionists in South Africa who, together with their American counterparts, were Israel's most enthusiastic supporters.[25]

ISRAEL'S WAR FOR WATER

Undeterred, in 1951, Israel moved bulldozers and military units into the de-militarised zone (DMZ) which had been created along the ceasefire line between Israel and Syria. This was strictly against the ceasefire agreement from 1949, according to which neither party was to deploy any military units inside the DMZ. Furthermore, the territory, a remnant of what had been Mandated Palestine, did not belong to either country, but was under United Nations (UN) control. Despite protests by UN observers, the Israelis began draining Lake Hula, which was part of the Jordan River system. Meanwhile, units of the Israeli Defence Force (IDF) began firing at Syrian villagers close to the ceasefire line. One of the UN observers, US Major-General A.R. Bolling, bitterly complained:

> [A]pparently, Israel is prepared to risk military operations against any of the Arab states, and several recent Israeli actions appear to have been designed, at least in part, to provoke Arab initiation of hostilities.

Nevertheless, the Syrians refused to get involved. While deploying some army units closer to the DMZ, they neither entered it nor fired back. The government of Jordan reacted in a different fashion. In mid-1952, it finalised its own scheme for development of the Jordan River (the so-called 'Bunger Plan') and convinced the US and the United Nations Relief and Works Agency for Palestine Refugees in the Near East (UNRWA) to earmark funds for the commencement of work on the Yarmouk River, a tributary of the Jordan. Israel, part of whose territory was situated lower down the river sytstem, objected to this plan. Correspondingly, allocation of US and UN funds was postponed.

Aware of two de-facto competing water schemes, the Eisenhower administration urged the UN to take the lead and develop a unified plan that would be acceptable to all the countries with riparian rights in the Jordan River system. Furthermore, the White House authorised the Tennessee Valley Authority to prepare a desk study that would synthesise the essential features of both Arab and Israeli planning.

However, on 2 September 1953, Israel began the rapid construction of a canal that would divert much of the water of the upper Jordan into Israel from a point near B'not Yaakov Bridge, inside the DMZ neighbouring Syria. The UN protested, but the Israelis only accelerated work on their canal. Syria then brought the matter to the UN Security Council (UNSC). This finally prompted a reaction from the US government. After all, Eisenhower had forced Jordan to stop its work, while the Israelis not only ignored his and UN requests to do the same, but also used US aid to finance their work, then breached the armistice agreement by entering the DMZ and opening fire at Syrian citizens. Without a satisfactory response from Israel, on 18 September 1953, the US administration stopped all US economic aid to Israel. One month later, the Israeli government agreed to stop work on the diversion project, promising it would cooperate with the UNSC's efforts to reach a solution that would take into account the legitimate rights of all riparian states. However, as soon as US aid resumed, Israel completed its unilateral water project – to no small degree with the help of money that had saved the country from bankruptcy in 1953. This had been German restitution for the Holocaust.[26] Thus began what was in practice part one of the Water War between Israel and its neighbours, a conflict that not only caused many attacks into Israel but which continues in various forms to this day.

CROSS-BORDER RAIDS

Preoccupied with the massive undertaking of securing himself in power in the face of opposition from Naguib and the Moslem Brotherhood, with modernising his country and improving its economy, in negotiations with Great Britain and the USA, fully understanding the realities of Egypt's military position vis-à-vis Israel, and faced with refusals from all possible sources to provide him with modern arms, Nasser had no interest in fighting another war with Egypt's new neighbour. Indeed, although no Arab leader could dare be known as anything less than a bitter enemy of Israel, in the course of his discussions with CIA operatives in Egypt, Nasser had not only been very flexible on the subject of Israel, but had even expressed his tolerance and respect.[27] Thus, when forced to face another crisis in this relationship, he reacted with constraint.

One of most critical issues between the Arab states and Israel in the early 1950s was that of illegal activity over the armistice lines of the Palestine War. Between 1949 and 1967, these largely coincided with the international frontier between Egypt and Palestine before the war of 1948-1949, except for the Gaza Strip and a DMZ further south. Egyptian Army units thus patrolled their side of the ceasefire line, not only between Egypt and Israel but also inside what had become known as the Gaza Strip, a small corner of Arab Palestine preserved by the Egyptian Army at the end of the Palestine War.

The majority of cross-border activities – and their number ran into thousands – were related to Palestinian refugees (civilians who either fled or had been expelled from their villages during the First Arab-Israeli War) attempting to access the land they lost as a result of the Palestine War. Israel insisted on indiscriminately designating all of them as terrorists, regardless of the fact that the vast majority of the civilians in question were never armed. Correspondingly, any related activities – armed or not, and whether or not they resulted in attacks on Israeli citizens or their possessions – were reported as terrorist attacks. Not only the IDF, but above all the government of Prime Minister David Ben-Gurion, declared that all such 'attacks' were launched by the Egyptian, Jordanian, Lebanese and Syrian militaries, or at least with the consent of those governments. Furthermore, Israel began publishing wildly exaggerated figures about the damage these incursions caused.[28] This inevitably created the impression that Israel was under near-constant and murderous attack by its neighbours.

In reality, as confirmed not only by dozens of contemporary accounts, but also by a host of documents released by Israeli sources since that time, all four Arab governments followed the policy of strictly curbing such activity. This was not only because they opposed a non-negotiated return of Palestinians into Israel, but more so because they were keen to prevent another war.[29] However, while the Lebanese and Syrian governments proved successful in their efforts – primarily because of the short armistice lines they shared with Israel – the Egyptians and Jordanians had far more problems. Principal amongst these was a lack of troops necessary to control hundreds of thousands of Palestinian refugees settled close to lengthy armistice lines, often only a few metres outside what had become Israel. Furthermore, Egyptian efforts to bring the situation under control were actually hampered by the terms of the armistice agreement of 1949, which strictly limited the number of Egyptian Army troops deployed in the Gaza Strip.[30]

In an attempt to bring the situation under control, in December 1952, the Egyptian RCC created the Palestinian Border Police. Between December 1952 and December 1953, three groups of trainees for this police and for a separate Saharti Battalion were recruited and underwent three months of training. Armed with weapons made in Great Britain, all were put under the command of Egyptian officers and other ranks, and had the primary purpose of restraining infiltrations into Israel.

SECRET PEACE NEGOTIATIONS

As could have been expected, the small contingent of Palestinian police proved hopelessly insufficient for its task, even more so when the power struggle between the RCC and the Moslem Brotherhood spread into the Gaza Strip where the Islamist fundamentalists became the principal instigators of an increasing number of genuinely armed infiltrations into Israel in 1953. While this prompted Cairo to establish another Palestinian unit – the 11th Battalion Palestinian Border Guard (PBG), consisting of 700 troops armed with mortars and machine guns – the frequency of infiltration activity nevertheless increased, resulting in robberies and then armed attacks on Israeli troops and civilians.

Supposedly in an attempt to suppress such activity, in August 1953 the IDF established Unit 101, a commando company which specialised in cross-border raids. Before long, this unit became involved in a number of bloody operations, its most notorious attack being the Qibya raid of 14-15 October 1953. Ordered by Ben-Gurion, this resulted in IDF soldiers slaughtering 66 men, women and children, blowing up the local school, a mosque and a number of homes.

This massacre was not only universally condemned by the international community, but might have been one of reasons why Ben-Gurion decided to temporarily retire from public life in November the same year. His successor, Moshe Sharett, followed a policy of moderation and gradualism, believing that despite significant differences with the Arabs, peace was possible and diplomacy desirable. However, because Ben-Gurion was not pleased with Sharett's appointment, one of his last official acts as Prime Minister was to appoint two close friends and hardliners to top positions; Pinchas Lavon became Minister of Defence and Moshe Dayan the IDF Chief-of-Staff. Thus came into being one of the strangest periods in Israeli history, during which the Prime Minister was running secret negotiations with the most important Arab heads of state, the foremost being Nasser, while his military was launching repeated illegal attacks across the armistice lines into Egypt, Jordan and Syria.

LAVON AFFAIR

In early 1954, Sharett initiated clandestine contacts with Nasser (primarily via various European intermediaries). One of the first results of their negotiations was that Egypt allowed shipping to and from Israel to pass through the Suez Canal in February that same year. However, on 17 March 1954, an Israeli bus in Negev was ambushed by Palestinian infiltrators and 11 Israelis were killed. Israeli retaliation was nowhere near as restrained as that of Nasser. Without waiting for the outcome of a UN attempt to establish responsibility for this attack, Unit 101 struck into Jordan on 28 March and killed nine civilians at Nahalin.[31]

The raid on Nahalin and a series of ever more destructive night attacks by Unit 101 prompted London to threaten that Israel would have to fight both Britain and Jordan if it occupied any Jordanian territory. Even the US State Department warned Israel to stop such raids. Ben-Gurion, Lavon and Dayan thus decided to change their tactics by spoiling secret peace negotiations between Nasser and Sharett.[32] In June 1954, Modin, the Israeli military intelligence agency, activated a ring of agents in Cairo and ordered it to launch attacks against selected British and American targets. The Alexandria

An 'infiltrator/terrorist' caught by IDF border troops in 1954. (Mark Lepko Collection)

Israel's Minister of Defence, Pinchas Lavon, and Moshe Dayan in 1954. (Mark Lepko Collection)

post office was fire-bombed on 2 July, the United States Information Agency offices in Cairo and Alexandria were damaged by fires on 14 July, and on 23 July the group bombed the Cairo central post office and tried to set fire to the Rio Cinema in Alexandria.

The latter operation failed and a stateless Israeli named Philip Nathanson was arrested when a small phosphorous bomb detonated in his trouser pocket. Nathanson was hospitalised and then interrogated. His flat was searched, additional incendiary bombs were found and two accomplices were then arrested. On 2 August, the US Embassy security officer was invited to Cairo police headquarters and given a full briefing on progress in the investigation. Within a few weeks of the first arrests, the entire ring of 11 Israeli agents had been rolled up, only the two leaders managing to escape. Following a public trial, four of the Israelis (including two who had escaped) were sentenced to be hung, while six received prison terms and two were acquitted.

What became known as the 'Lavon Affair' was obviously an amateurish Israeli attempt to sabotage Egypt's relations with the United States and Britain which should have turned into another diplomatic disaster for Israel. The reason why this was not the case was a series of fateful events in late 1954 and 1955.

A group of Egyptian Army officers assigned to the garrison in Sudan in 1939. Nasser is standing first on the right, in the second row, with Amer to the left of the Egyptian national flag. (Bibliotheca Alexandrina)

2

THE TURNING POINT

In late 1954 and early 1955, Gamal Abdel Nasser found himself confronted with a host of massive tasks. In a matter of six months, he had to find a solution to his power struggle with Naguib and the Moslem Brotherhood, and for ongoing disputes with Western powers, while obtaining funding for construction of the Nile High Dam near Aswan. At the same time, and although negotiating peace with Israel, he found his country exposed to a series of Israeli cross-border raids that had humiliated the Egyptian military, which was the very backbone of the modern-day Egyptian state and of Nasser's rule. Meanwhile, his intelligence service was reporting that France was providing Israel with ever-increasing amounts of advanced armaments.

Facing the combination of an arms embargo imposed by Great Britain, being unable to source arms from elsewhere and aware of an existing qualitative and quantitative gap with the Israeli military, the President of Egypt was left with little choice but to make a number of fateful decisions within the shortest possible time.

ORIGINS OF THE EGYPTIAN MILITARY

The origins of the modern-day Egyptian military can be traced back to the army established during the reign of Muhammad Ali Pasha, the 'founder of modern Egypt', in the first half of the nineteenth century. Aiming to create a disciplined and indoctrinated military, the Pasha enforced conscription in 1822 and separated recruits from civilian life. He imposed a system of strict rules and regulations designed to keep troops busy and to develop a sense of respect for the law, while also placing them under close surveillance. The latter aspect was particularly important, because Egyptian soldiers had previously often ransacked nearby towns or villages, causing mayhem wherever they went. A combination of harsh punishment and a roll-call three times of day dispelled any thoughts of desertion

or dissent, and created a mindset of absolute obedience.

Once the British became embroiled in Egypt in 1882, they helped create a stable, economically sound country, but also one that could secure the protection of the British Empire's communications. Under British supervision, the Egyptian Army was reformed, modernised and restructured for operations on the modern battlefield. Amongst other things, further policies designed to instil discipline and a sense of collective solidarity in every soldier were introduced. The result of these measures was that over time, and despite its limitations, the Egyptian military developed into a comparatively efficient force, Western in professional outlook. It was also a force which reflected the military characteristics of cohesion and dedication – qualities relatively rare elsewhere in Egyptian public life.[1] To a certain degree, it can thus be said that Britain had created the instrument which was to establish modern-day Egypt and then enforced the demise of British Imperial influence upon the country and the Suez Canal.

The Egyptian military had been significantly expanded during the Palestine War, but remained equipped with haphazardly obtained arms of Western origin acquired by Cairo's representatives from whatever overseas sources were available. Immediately after the armistice of 1949, the Egyptian government allocated £52 million to 'build an army which will be one of the most formidable in the Middle East'.[2] Eager to create a British-Egyptian military partnership for the defence of the Middle East against Soviet aggression, London granted permission for the export of various weapons in 1950. However, because of the Tripartite Declaration and as a result of various Anglo-Egyptian negotiations, the British government embargoed most resulting Egyptian arms orders. London refused to move in this regards, even when Egyptian Prime Minister Nahas Pasha offered to support Britain in defence of the Middle East in exchange for arms in early 1951.[3]

Nowhere was this refusal more obvious than in orders for new equipment for the Royal Egyptian Air Force, nearly 50 percent of aircraft ordered in 1949, and more than 90 percent ordered in 1950, being impounded. Of about 350 aircraft that Egypt was permitted o order from Great Britain by August 1953, when most embargoes were temporarily lifted, less than 100 were actually delivered, and most of them were hopelessly obsolete. Some were not even armed. Another embargo prevented the Egyptians from opening a production line for Vampire jets in a newly constructed factory at Helwan, south of Cairo, although all the expensive machinery had been paid for and was already in place.[4] Supplies of spares were similarly intermittent and unpredictable, wreaking havoc with the REAF's training and expansion schedules.

THE GAZA RAID

Keen to stop all negotiations between Nasser and Sharett – but also to prompt Egypt to order a renewed closure of the Suez Canal for Israeli shipping and thus spoil ongoing negotiations between Cairo, Washington and London – Ben-Gurion, Lavon and Dayan ordered another series of cross-border raids by Unit 101.[5] Undertaken between 22 August and 3 September 1954, most of these took the Arabs by surprise and they were unable to respond in any other fashion than through indirect measures. On 28 September, an Israeli owned ship, *Bat Galim*, was seized while approaching the southern side of the Suez Canal, allegedly for firing on Egyptian fishermen in the Gulf of Suez. The canal was thus once again blocked for Israeli shipping.

However, during the same month, the Egyptian Army also established two new Palestinian battalions – the 32nd and 43rd. As soon as these were operational, they were combined with the existing 11th Battalion into the 86 Brigade of what was now officially the Palestine Border Guards. Deployed along the armistice lines, their task was to curb infiltrations into Israel. Ben-Gurion then authorised a massive IDF attack against the Egyptian military presence in the Gaza Strip. On the evening of 27 February 1955, Unit 101 killed 39 Egyptian soldiers, including a captain, in their beds. When another Egyptian unit rushed to the scene, it lost seven or eight soldiers killed and 29 injured.

What became colloquially known as the 'Gaza Raid' proved to be a turning point. It not only forced Nasser into a realisation that a negotiated settlement of the Arab-Israeli dispute was impossible without complete Arab surrender, but led him to expect a new war with Israel. His humiliated and now enraged military was clearly in need of new arms.

ARMS RACE

There is still controversy about whether or not the Gaza Raid prompted Nasser's decision to rearm Egypt – a decision widely considered as crucial for the outbreak of the Suez War. The Egyptian version is that Nasser had sincere intentions to establish good relations with the West and to negotiate with Israel, but was forced into ordering arms by the behaviour of Western powers and Israel, especially by the IDF's attack on the Gaza Strip. According to that version of events, Nasser's search for arms led him to a meeting with Chou En-Lai, Prime Minister of the People's Republic of China, in April 1955, during the Afro-Asian summit in Bandung, Indonesia. When asked if China would sell arms to Egypt, Chou recommended Nasser to request these directly from the Soviet Union, and promised to take the matter up with Moscow. Furthermore, meetings with other leaders from around the world supposedly broadened Nasser's horizons and inspired him to take a new direction in his foreign policy. Again according to this version, Nasser then received a positive reply in April 1955 via the Soviet ambassador to Cairo, Daniel Solod, who reportedly informed him that the USSR was also prepared to help Egypt finance the High

The foreign policy of Soviet leader Nikita Khrushchev was fundamentally different to that of his predecessor Stalin, and would result in a number of serious confrontations with Western powers during the late 1950s and early 1960s. (Mark Lepko Collection)

Dam at Aswan.

According to most Israeli versions, however, there was no connection between the Gaza Raid (if this is mentioned at all) and Nasser's quest for arms, and Israel was therefore not to blame. On the contrary, Nasser's decision was supposedly related to long-established Egyptian ambitions. Some of the better-informed narratives concerning this question are based upon documentation declassified from Czech archives over the last 20 years. According to this version, Cairo contracted Moscow and Prague as early as 1951 and placed several orders for arms.

However, the fact is that while these talks were held, all were fruitless. Soviet leader Joseph Vissarionovich Stalin did not want to become involved in the Middle East for fear of British retaliation. Furthermore, the involved Soviet officials regarded, perhaps correctly, Egyptian requests as attempts to play the Soviets against the British. Correspondingly, when the mission deployed by Nahas Pasha visited Prague, in October 1951, and requested delivery of 200 tanks and 200 other armoured vehicles, 60-100 MiG-15s, 2,000 trucks and 1,000 jeeps, the Czechoslovak government informed them that for various reasons, it would not be able to meet this request. Almost exactly the same happened when Naguib sent another delegation to Prague in 1952 and one to Moscow in early 1953.[6]

The situation began to change with the rise to power of Stalin's successor, Nikita Sergeyevich Khrushchev, in 1953. Khrushchev not only abandoned the old policy of considering all non-communist countries as enemies, but decided to play a more active role in the Middle East and encouraged the Czechoslovak government to strengthen its ties with Egypt. However, even then, the visit of another Egyptian delegation in Moscow, in April 1954, proved fruitless, and it was only in August that year that the Soviets signalled their preparedness for serious negotiations.[7]

A cross-reference of information from Western sources with documentation from Czechoslovak archives confirms that it was the

Israeli raid on Gaza in late February 1955 that motivated Nasser to launch a major effort to obtain modern armaments. It also indicates that Nasser was discouraged by earlier negotiations with the Soviets and Czechoslovaks. In fact, early in 1955, he opened secret negotiations with Great Britain and the USA, requesting not only arms but above all help with financing the High Dam at Aswan.[8]

The USA and Great Britain reacted with an offer to help finance construction of the High Dam with a loan of US $270 million, and the Americans also expressed a preparedness to sell some arms – but on their usual conditions, which included Egypt joining an anti-Soviet alliance. Nasser countered with requests of his own, most of which proved unacceptable for the West. Negotiations dragged on without the parties getting any nearer a common accord. In an attempt to find a solution, British Prime Minister Anthony Eden – an Arabic speaker who considered himself sympathetic towards the Arabs, had never supported Zionism and had welcomed the expulsion of King Farouq – visited Egypt in January 1955. However, on arrival in Cairo, he behaved towards Nasser in a patronising fashion by inviting the Egyptian President to the British Embassy. Unsurprisingly, Eden's greeting in flawless Arabic left Nasser unimpressed. The Egyptian strongman only expressed his hostility to the proposed METO (Middle Eastern Treaty Organisation) and explained his concerns that the West was attempting to draw the Arab world into the Cold War.[9]

While Nasser was confident he could make a deal with the USA as late as March-April 1955, it remains unknown whether these negotiations would really have resulted in a solution. There were three main reasons for this. Firstly, the British leaked some details about related talks to the press, which embarrassed Nasser. Secondly, an Egyptian initiative failed to create an alternative security pact involving Syria and Saudi Arabia, which had the potential of putting him in a strong bargaining position in negotiations with Washington. Thirdly, Egyptian intelligence assessments suggested that Britain and America were behind Israeli actions such as the Gaza Raid, and that this was a part of a US plan to isolate Egypt on the international scene.[10] All of this resulted in President Nasser making the acquisition of Soviet arms his priority.

LATE MYSTÈRES

Another frequently narrated Israeli and Western version is that it was only in reaction to the Egyptian arms deals with the USSR that Israel began placing large orders for arms from France. Such opinions are supported by the fact that most of the jet fighters made in France and deployed by the IDF/AF (Israeli Defence Force/Air Force) during the Suez War had only been ordered by Israel after the spring of 1955, and that most of them were delivered only in 1956. At first glance, this theory is perfectly correct.

However, since 1951, France had de-facto replaced the USA as Israel's primary sponsor and had begun selling ever larger amounts of weaponry – primarily tanks and other vehicles initially. There is little doubt that Washington welcomed such activity. Although most Israeli purchases were sponsored with funds provided by private contributions from Jewish communities in the USA, they suited Truman's and then Eisenhower's administrations perfectly because they satisfied Israel's security concerns without jeopardising US relations with the Arab world. Unsurprisingly, the USA did nothing when France and Israel even entered cooperation in the field of nuclear research, which subsequently led them to cooperate regarding the development of nuclear weapons.[11]

Because the French aircraft industry was still recovering from the damage caused by the Second World War, it could not immediately

One of eleven Meteor F.Mk 8s acquired by the IDF/AF, starting in 1953. Four of these were originally manufactured for Egypt. (Albert Grandolini Collection)

A Sabre that was not to be: a Canadian-built F-86F in camouflage colours and markings of the IDF/AF. (Albert Grandolini Collection)

offer advanced fighter jets. Therefore, the first significant deal between Israel and France concerning the IDF/AF, signed in February 1951, was for delivery of 63 De Havilland Mosquito fighter-bombers from surplus stocks of the Armée de l'Air (French Air Force, AdA). Following overhauls in France, 58 of these reached Israel, thus significantly bolstering the IDF/AF's existing fleet of North American P-51D Mustangs, Supermarine Spitfires of several different marks and North American T-6 Texans. Quantitatively, such a fleet was neither superior nor weaker than that of the REAF. However, because of the free flow of spares from the USA and elsewhere, and the continuous presence of foreign instructors, the Israelis experienced far fewer problems in training additional pilots than did the Egyptians. In practice, curbs to their operations only stemmed from the dire economic situation of Israel. Indeed, most available accounts about the history of the IDF/AF stress that it was during the early 1950s that the Chief-of-Staff IDF/AF, Dan Tolkovsky, laid the foundations for the modern-day Israeli air force.

There is no doubt that Israel was second to Egypt in the adoption of jet fighters. This process began in February 1953, when the British government granted permission for a delivery of 11 Gloster Meteor F.Mk 8s and four T.Mk 7s, plus conversion training for Israeli pilots in the United Kingdom. The first two of these aircraft reached Ramat David AB (air base) in June the same year. While embargoing one Egyptian request after another around this time, the British government showed less reluctance in granting permission for another Israeli order, this time for seven Meteor FR.Mk 9s and two additional T.Mk 7s in March 1954, delivery of which was completed in May 1955.

By then, the IDF/AF had become involved in a much more significant deal with France – one that raised enough attention in Egypt to influence Nasser's decision to search for arms. Namely, starting in mid-1953, the IDF/AF decided to obtain swept-wing jet

Original choice: a rare photograph of a MD.452 Mystère II in service with the Escadre de Chasse 10 (EC.10) of the French Air Force (Armée de l'Air, Ada). Essentially a stretched variant of the Ouragan with swept but thick wings, this type was quickly superseded by the much more advanced Mystère IVA. (Albert Grandolini Collection)

Postponements in development of the Mystère II led to Israel eventually placing an order for much better Mystère IVAs in 1955. This is one of the first four examples delivered in 1956. (Albert Grandolini Collection)

fighters.[12]

Israel's original preference was for the North American F-86 Sabre. However, the Eisenhower administration insisted on maintaining the Tripartite Declaration and ruled out any such sales. Undeterred, the Israelis began searching elsewhere and ended up flight-testing the SAAB J29 Tunnan in Sweden and the Dassault MD.452 Mystère II in France. The Tunnan was already in operational service, while the Mystère II was still under development, but promised to offer generally superior performance. Nevertheless, the IDF/AF rejected both types, and continued its attempts to acquire Canadair-manufactured F-86s. Only once this solution was blocked by the State Department in July 1954, did Israel finally place an order for Mystère IIs. The contract was signed on 23 August 1954, and stipulated delivery of six MD.452s (and a single Nord 2501 Noratlas transport aircraft), with an option for a further nine Mystères and two Noratlases.[13] The original delivery date for the first batch of Mystère IIs built for Israel was scheduled for February-March 1955.

Further development of this type encountered numerous problems. These were so serious that delivery was first rescheduled for July 1955, and then postponed ever further. Indeed, during the summer of 1955, the French had no other option but to offer the Israelis a batch of 12 Dassault MD.450 Ouragans as a stop-gap measure, until the first 12 Mystère IIs would be finally available. After studying this offer, in September the same year, the IDF/AF eventually accepted the offer of Ouragans, but cancelled the purchase of Mystère IIs and instead placed an order for more advanced Mystère IVs, for delivery in 1956.

Therefore, while there is no doubt that – contrary to reports by Egyptian military intelligence from late 1954 – the Israelis did not start receiving any new French-made fighter jets before 1956, there is also no doubt that it was the Israeli order for swept-wing fighters

from July 1954 that set off alarm bells in Cairo; the more so because at that time the EAF not only had no comparable fighter jets in service, but also had no allies from whom to source such advanced aircraft.

In essence, Egypt and Israel were henceforth in a race to absorb their new military equipment. As time would show, while Egypt was only trying to secure herself against an attack from an aggressive neighbour, Israel was intensively preparing for an invasion of Egypt.[14]

3
EGYPTIAN AIR FORCE OF 1954-1955

The REAF was originally established in 1932 as the Egyptian Army Air Force, and became an independent branch of the military in 1937. Always restricted by what the British were willing to deliver, and what the government of King Farouq was ready to pay for or could afford, it saw little involvement in the Second World War, but distinguished itself during the Palestine War, although lacking experienced pilots and modern equipment.

For a short while after the Egyptian Revolution of 1952, King Farouq's young son remained the nominal ruler of the country, and thus the service retained its prefix Royal until the monarchy was finally abolished in June 1953. Nevertheless, important personnel changes were introduced at a much earlier date.

NEW CHIEF-OF-STAFF

As early as 23 July 1952, the RCC made the politically understandable, but professionally unwise and arbitrary decision to retire not only the Chief of Staff REAF, Mohammed Mustafa Sha'arawy, but also all officers above the rank of wing commander. They were all forced into early retirement, with the exception of a handful of officers who were considered 'cronies' of King Farouq and were forced to leave the country entirely. Because only one REAF officer who was also a member of the Free Officers Movement had yet reached sufficient rank, this move removed all those with senior staff experience. The exceptions were Wing Commanders Abd el-Latif Boghdadi and Ali Sabri. Both were veterans of the Palestine War, Boghdadi then becoming CO of Heliopolis AB while Sabri became Chief of REAF Intelligence

The availability of an experienced and proven officer like

Boghdadi might make the next decision by the RCC appear strange. This is even more so considering the fact that the selection of another officer instead of Boghdadi was not only because he had studiously avoided involvement in politics, but also because the officer in question had many years of good relations with the Royal Air Force (RAF), a fact which recommended him as somebody likely to improve relations with Great Britain. This officer was Air Commodore Hassan Mahmoud, another highly experienced and competent veteran of the Palestine War.

However, the RCC was quick to conclude that attempts to improve relations with Britain based upon mutual respect were a pipe dream. Despite subsequent statements indicating something entirely different, London showed not the least willingness to accept and understand Egyptian interests, and thus to improve its relations with the new Egypt. As a result, Mahmoud was recalled to Cairo from Britain and took over command of the REAF.

Perfectly aware of the importance of recruiting and training, Mahmoud launched a substantial recruitment drive in early 1953, with the intention of training an entirely new generation of pilots and support personnel. However, his efforts misfired, as while there were more than enough volunteers, plenty of enthusiasm and eagerness to learn, there were very few experienced instructors and -- as will become clear – even fewer suitable training aircraft.

POST-REVOLUTIONARY PURGES

The power struggle between Nasser, Neguib and the Moslem Brotherhood resulted in a further purge of the air force in 1953. This removed nearly all officers loyal to the first Egyptian President plus most of those suspected of having links with fundamentalists or communists. In their place, the RCC began imposing officers promoted for political loyalty, rather than professional competence. Sadly, this was one of the first signs of what would become endemic in the 1960s. Disappointed by such decisions, Hassan Mahmoud resigned. In his place, on 23 June 1953, the RCC appointed Mahmoud Sidki Mahmoud – known to his friends and colleagues by his nickname 'Uncle Hamada' – as the new Chief-of-Staff of what was now the Egyptian Air Force (EAF).

A bomber pilot during the Palestine War, Sidki Mahmoud had served as CO of Dikhelia AB in the early 1950s, and then commanded the Air Force College from December 1951 until July 1952. Unlike Hassan Mahmoud, Sidki Mahmoud was considered as having fingers in several political pies, although – until the Egyptian Revolution – it was never clear whether he might have been a royalist, sympathetic to the British or some other country or body.

Even during this purge, there were curious exceptions such as that of Kamal Zaki. With his great-grandfather having served in the Khedive's government during the nineteenth century, and a grandfather having been an officer in the Egyptian Army of the 1890s (at the time of the Anglo-Egyptian reconquest of Mahdist Sudan), he was considered a possible royalist. However, he was permitted to continue serving, together with a few others with similar links.

Some other officers survived under even more surprising circumstances. One example was that of Group-Captain Hassan Tewfik, an enterprising technical officer who played a crucial role in establishing Egypt's first radar station during the Palestine War. Although taking his officer's oath of loyalty to the Egyptian Crown very seriously, Tewfik regarded King Farouq as a highly dubious character. Nevertheless, he was shocked by fellow officers who took part in or accepted the coup. Some were amongst his best friends, but despite his openly expressed criticism of their actions, they remained close, accepting that each individual must follow his own conscience. However, when Nasser once publicly accused senior, retired officers as being 'useless, thieves and traitors', Tewfik became so incensed that he contacted Nasser personally and said, 'If you refer to me, refer to me as useless, but not as a traitor to my country!' Much to Nasser's credit, he accepted Tewfik's outburst and subsequently placed him in charge of Egypt's missile development programme.

That said, and generally speaking, those EAF officers who continued serving after early 1954 were either considered loyal to the revolution or were amongst those who kept their political opinions strictly to themselves.

Other changes within the EAF in the period 1952-1954 were more of a cosmetic rather than fundamental nature. One of these was Nasser's order for the air force (and navy) to replace its traditional, British-influenced ranking stripes with those of the army's stars and eagles. While the navy simply refused (at least in regards of their sleeves, because this system was internationally recognised), the air force accepted and thus readopted the ranks which had been used in the 1930s. Nevertheless, many REAF officers from this period continued thinking of themselves in what Egyptians called 'air force style ranks'. This is why such ranks are given in this book. Similarly, and despite increasing nationalist feelings everywhere within Egypt, the EAF clung to its British, RAF-style way of doing things.

RECRUITMENT AND TRAINING

A combination of the British arms embargoes and the RCC's insistence on maintaining an existing command structure in the Egyptian military – which resulted in the air force being de-facto subject to the control of the army – conspired to prevent the EAF from obtaining the equipment, installations and personnel necessary to improve its training.

For example, applicants for entry into the Air Force College at Bilbeis AB had first to undergo two years of training at the Army's Military Academy, with at most three familiarisation flights during that time, before eventually coming under the tutelage of the EAF. As of the early 1950s, the Egyptian air force was accepting candidates for the Air Force College as young as 16 or 17. They could also be up to 24 years of age if they already had a university degree. However, once at the Military Academy, many candidates were head-hunted by the Army, and it often took personal interventions on the part of commanders of the Air Force College to convince applicants for the air force to continue serving with the EAF. Unsurprisingly, for many years, successive commanders of the Air Force College – especially Madkour Abu al-Ezz and Muhammad Hosni Mubarak, the future President of Egypt – became some of the most important officers of the air force.[1]

After completing two years of training at the Military Academy, EAF cadets were thrown headlong into flying training and expected to learn to fly solo after only 20 flying hours. Combined with the fact that the principal basic trainers in service in the early 1950s were Miles Magisters – designed and produced back in the 1930s – and that the EAF was chronically short of experienced instructor pilots, this resulted in a significant number of accidents.

During the summer of 1953, relations between Egypt and Great Britain improved enough for London to partially ease the arms embargo and grant permission for the acquisition of jet fighters. Sidki Mahmoud and one of his most experienced pilots, Mustafa Abu Zaid, also exploited this opportunity to negotiate the purchase of 22 De Havilland Canada Chipmunk basic trainers from Canada.[2]

Ultimately, the problem with a lack of basic trainers was only solved in 1955, when Factory 72 in Heliopolis started producing

The obligatory start of every pilot's career in Egypt in the early 1950s as elsewhere included extensive medical checks. (Nour Bardai Collection)

Mustafa Abu Zaid the pilot who was crucial in the acquisition and introduction into service of the Chipmunk in Egypt inside the cockpit of one of the Canadian-built primary trainers. (Muhammad Abu Zaid Collection)

The primary trainer of the EAF in the early 1950s was still the hopelessly obsolete Miles Magister. (David Nicolle Collection)

About 20 T-6 Texan/Harvards sourced from around the world were in service with the EAF in 1956. Most were painted yellow. (David Nicolle Collection)

A rare photograph of an EAF Chipmunk (serial number 1650). Egypt had purchased more than 50 of these by 1956. (de Havilland Canada, via David Nicolle)

Gomhouriya ('Republic') T.Mk 1 primary trainers. Based on the design of the German Bücker Bü.181D Bestman from the Second World War, and originally intended to be called the Farukiyah (after King Farouq), this project had been launched in 1950, with support from Czechoslovakia.

Acquisition of modern advanced trainers proved a much more problematic issue. As of 1953, the Air Force College used North AmericanT-6 Texans for such purposes. The story of that type's service in Egypt began in July 1943, when the RAF's No. 71 Operational Training Unit (OTU) lent two Harvards to the REAF's Flying School at Almaza AB. From then and until the end of the Second World War, the RAF loaned Harvards in ones or twos to the REAF whenever the British authorities felt able – or inclined – to do so. It was only in 1946 that the REAF was permitted to purchase Harvards from surplus RAF stocks in the Middle East.

According to a contemporary report by the British Parliament,

The second Fury FB.Mk 11 delivered to Egypt received the serial number 702. Here it is at Almaza post-delivery, together with Neville Duke (in suit) and Squadron Leader Raouf the CO of No. 1 Squadron, REAF. Note the application of identification stripes, national markings and serial numbers on bottom wing surfaces. (Neville Duke Collection, via David Nicolle)

Inside Factory 72 at Helwan, showing the final assembly of the 12th series example of the Gomhouriya Mk.1 basic trainer. (Nour Bardai Collection)

The same aircraft seen during a pre-delivery flight over Egypt. (Neville Duke Collection, via David Nicolle)

A scan from The Armed Forces Magazine, showing one of the early Gomhouriya Mk. 1 basic trainers. (Nour Bardai Collection)

about 20 T-6s were sold to Egypt between May 1945 and June 1947. The REAF usually kept 12 of these operational, although sometimes more were in service, depending on requirements. For example, in late 1949, when the Flying Training School at Almaza moved to the newly constructed Air Force College in Bilbeis, the REAF reported having ten Harvards in operational condition and eight in reserve.[3] A few additional examples must have been obtained subsequently from diverse sources, because 12 serviceable and 12 unserviceable Harvards were reported on strength at the Air College in 1952. However, when Sidki Mahmoud attempted to place an order for 15 Canadian-built Harvards in 1953, the British embargoed their delivery, arguing that they could also be used for ground-attack. Thefefore, it was only in 1955 that this order was finally granted permission to be converted into a contract, and 15 Harvards were shipped to Egypt from Nova Scotia. The Canadian government also sold nine Harvards to Egypt on 8 March 1956.

Therefore, during the period 1953-1955, the Egyptians were forced to start making use of older piston-engined fighters – including worn-out Fiat G.55s and Aer Macchi MC.205s – for advanced training purposes. Another type still available in significant numbers was the Supermarine Spitfire, with 19 F.Mk 22s and a single Spitfire

The first Spitfire F.Mk 22 for Egypt, as seen prior to delivery, following an overhaul by Vickers. The total worth of the deal for nineteen F.Mk 22s and one T.Mk 9 was £239,000, and these Spitfires remained in service. (Photo by R. Arnold, via David Nicolle)

One of nineteen Supermarine Spitfire F.Mk 22s ordered by the Royal Egyptian Air Force on 1 May 1950, as seen during a stop at Luqa, Malta, in late 1950. (Photo by N. Lees, via David Nicolle)

Since 1952, surviving Fiat G.55 fighters had been relegated to an advanced training role, and few might have been in service as of 1956. They had an overall bare metal finish with 'trainer yellow' bands around the rear fuselage, with black serials (1251 in this case on a two-seater G55B) on the fuselage band. The last two digits of the serial were often repeated on the lower wing surface, inside the wingtip band. (Nour Bardai Collection)

T.Mk 9 being acquired in 1950-1951. By 1953, all served with the Fighter Conversion Unit (FCU), based at Almaza. In early 1955, when el-Arish-based No. 31 Squadron converted to jet-powered de Havilland Vampire FB.Mk 52s, the FCU was further reinforced by survivors of the 11 Hawker Sea Furies acquired in 1953.

FOREIGN INSTRUCTORS

Finding no quick solution for its lack of qualified instructors, the EAF – many of whose officers remained keen to maintain contacts with their RAF counterparts both professional and social – requested help from Great Britain. Because senior Egyptian military commanders and political leaders, not to mention the British themselves, proved far less enthusiastic, the resulting negotiations only bore fruit in late 1954 following the successful conclusion of negotiations for the withdrawal of British troops from Egypt. The EAF then requested 20 ex-RAF pilots to be seconded on a temporary basis to serve as instructors. Only six eventually turned up and proved suitable, including pilots named Hunt, Brisk, Sharp, Hatfield, Larcombe and a man known as 'Lion' (although this might have been a nickname for Larcombe). They arrived in Bilbeis in October 1955 and were horrified to find old-fashioned but also very unorthodox methods being used. The Air Force College lacked almost everything, including flying clothes. Cadets were being pushed through too quickly, going straight from North American T-6 Harvard trainers to jet conversion courses, and most of the Egyptian instructors had relatively little experience. A pilot with 900 hours was considered an expert.

Flight Lieutenants Sindey Brisk and David Larcombe recalled their impressions upon arrival in Egypt in October 1955:

When we got to Bilbeis, we found a fairly reasonable assembly of training aircraft: about 15 Gomhouriyas, some 25 Chipnunks and 20 Harvards. We were told, 'Whatever you do, don't try to spin the Chipmunk, we have already lost three of them in spins; it is an impossible manoeuvre.' This intrigued us, and so, of course, as soon as we got into the air in one we duly spun it. No trouble at all. The Egyptians were horrified. In fact, so convinced were they that there was something basically wrong with all Chipmunks that they called for the de Havilland representative from England to 'put it right'. After a searching investigation he reported, 'There is nothing wrong with the Chipmunk; it is the Egyptian pilots. They never get into a spin properly and they have no idea how to get out of one.' We set to work to try and instil a little basic knowledge into our new pupils. They were nice enough fellows on the whole – most spoke English – very polite, kind, and very eager to get into the class under a British instructor. 'Now we will really learn to fly,' they said. Unfortunately they never did. Their intelligence was not on a level with their keenness, and their retentive powers were almost nil. They forgot tomorrow what they had been taught today. And above all was their stubborn indifference to the niceties of flying; they didn't care whether they executed a manoeuvre well or badly as long as they somehow got the machine into the air and got down again in one piece.

What the ex-RAF instructor pilots did not know was that the EAF ordered 12 de Havilland Vampire T.Mk 55 advanced jet trainers, necessary to convert additional pilots to future jets, in the spring of 1955. However, as so often before, the British obstructed the sale on the grounds that these could be used in combat. After additional negotiations, London eventually allowed the sale and all 12 Vampires were delivered by 3 March 1956. But immediately afterwards, even the sale of ex-RAF stocks of bombs and drop tanks from redundant stocks stored in the Canal Zone was blocked on the grounds that such equipment would make defensive aircraft into offensive ones.

All British personnel appear to have left by early 1956. Although there are rumours that at least the pilot named Sharp was still flying Hawker Furies with the Fighter Training Unit (FTU) at the time of the 1956 war, this remains doubtful.[4] In fact, the Egyptians generally got on better with a number of ex-Indian Air Force instructors, who arrived to replace the British. Indeed, Indians were to play a crucial role in the basic training of hundreds of future Egyptian pilots for at least another decade.

For all these reasons, the EAF class of 1955 was still in training

Co-author Gabr Ali Gabr climbing into the rear cockpit of a T-6 at the Air Force College in January 1954. (Gabr Ali Gabr Collection)

Abdel Moneim el-Shennawy seen on the day he successfully completed his conversion course on a Vampire FB.Mk 52. As well as the last two figures of the aircraft's serial number ('22' from 1522), note the launch rails for unguided rockets, installed near the wing roots. (el-Shennawy Collection)

when the Suez War erupted. Nevertheless, it included men who would play a significant role in later wars against Israel. Also, the next generation of future Egyptian officers and pilots would be strongly influenced in their decision to join the EAF by developments during 1956.

EAF GENERATIONS 1954-1956

Many of the Egyptian pilots who became involved in the Suez War were novices who had only graduated at the Air Force College in 1954. Among them was this volume's co-author, Gabr Ali Gabr:

I was born on 12 March 1932, into a family of landowners in the Nile Delta, and still in the secondary school when I volunteered for the armed services, during the Palestine War. I was refused because still only 16 years old, but then the Military Academy had been opened and I was one of the first to enter. I graduated while aged 19 and was nominally reassigned to the air force, but remained at the Military Academy for a further year. In 1952, I went to the Air Force College, from which I graduated on 1 July 1955.

At the Air Force College, I first flew Chipmunks and then Harvards, with one year on each. Hosni Mubarak belonged to the staff and was one of my instructors on Chipmunks. We also had cadets from Saudi Arabia and Somalia with us. One of the Saudis was very small and experienced similar problems as I did: we were too small to fly the Harvard comfortably. My Harvard instructor was Bahig Hamza, an ex-Meteor F.Mk 8 pilot.

Tahsin Zaki (second from right) with colleagues and a Spitfire F.Mk 22 at el-Arish AB in 1953. (Tahsin Zaki Collection)

Although of poor quality, this photograph is highly interesting for showing top EAF flight instructors at the Air Force College in the mid-1950s, in front of two Spitfire F.Mk 22s. Among them are Hosni Mubarak (standing, second from right), Muhammad Kamil al-Mawawy (standing, sixth from right) and Shalabi el-Hinnawy (seated, second from left). (via Dr Abdallah Emran)

After graduating, I was assigned to the Fighter Training Unit at Almaza, then commanded by Musallam Nofall, and taught to fly the Vampire T.Mk 55. In December 1955, I was posted to No. 31 Squadron which, together with No. 1 Squadron, was equipped with Vampires and based at Kabrit.

All our training missions were flown over Sinai, mostly over the northern part of the peninsula, but one of my first training sorties – indeed, my first flight from el-Arish – was over or around southern Sinai, at an altitude of 30,000ft, then dropping to very low level across the armistice-line and into the Israeli-controlled Negev. Most of our training consisted of practicing reconnaissance and ground-attack missions. I never exercised air combat nor air-to-air gunnery before undergoing conversion course for MiGs in Czechoslovakia a few years later.

Fuad Kamal graduated with Gabr and then qualified to fly Meteors. He joined No. 20 Squadron, which at the time was commanded by his half-brother, Kamal Zaki, in 1956.[5] Graduating with Gabr Ali Gabr and Fuad Kamal was Abdel Moneim el-Shennawy. His son, Tarek, recalled his father's early career:

My father was born on 9 July 1931, in Nefia, a village in the Nile Delta, 3km away from Tanta. He was the seventh from eight brothers. His father died on 2 July 1938, but his mother took great care of the family and raised her children to excellent positions. Her second son graduated as an engineer, became a major general in the Army and was later responsible for agricultural development of the Nile Delta. Together with a cousin, my father joined the air force in July 1951. He graduated in July 1954 and was based at Almaza AB, flying Vampires from 1955 until 1957.

Entries in el-Shennawy's logbook show that he underwent training at the Air Force Academy from 1 October 1951 until 25 September 1954. His first flight was on a de Havilland Canada Chipmunk on 11 October 1952 and he flew his first solo on 17 November 1952. By the time of his graduation, el-Shennawy had accumulated a total of 213 hours. He then completed his advanced training phase, flying T-6 Harvards, before entering a conversion course for Meteors (completed with a solo flight on 30 April 1955) and Vampires (completed with a solo flight on 4 May 1955, when he flew serial number 1528). By 29 August 1956, el-Shennawy had accumulated a total of 250 hours, and subsequently flew a number of combat sorties during the Suez War.

A large group of younger pilots graduated in 1956. Amongst them was Ala'a Barakat, who subsequently qualified to fly Meteors with No. 20 Squadron before being reassigned to No. 5 Squadron at Fayid. Another was Adil Nasser, who converted to Vampires at the FTU at Kabrit only days before the Suez War broke out. In contrast, Abd al-Moneim at-Tawil joined the air force too late to fly in combat during that conflict:

I had been interested in aircraft as a boy and when I was 16, I joined the Air Force College, in 1955. There were no problems: I just went straight in, and qualified after six months at the Military Academy – though some of the students were later washed out at Bilbeis.

Tawil clearly recalled Brisk and Larcombe, who were 'considered a bit crazy', and certainly not regarded with awe. One had reputedly been expelled from the RAF for rolling a Lancaster, while Larcombe constantly chattered over the intercom and seemed to have had his nerves shattered by previous service in the RAF. Tawil continued:

After my basic training, I went on to the Harvard. We thought that the Harvards had very large cockpits, probably because they were designed for Americans. In fact, I found it hard to press the brake on the rudder pedals because they were so far away. Braking on the Chipmuk was easier because it was done by hand. We had student pilots from other countries too. That was before Sudan was fully independent and so they sent their pilots to train in Egypt. The Sudanese had a reputation for forgetting to lower their undercarriages.

Another of my instructors at Bilbais was Tahsin Zaki, who later served as squadron and then base commander. Our training and graduation had been held up because of the Suez War, and thus I graduated – on the Harvard – and got my wings only in 1957.

From left to right: Fikri Zahir, Taher Zaki, Musallam Nofall and an unknown pilot, after arriving in Egypt with a brand-new Meteor F.Mk 4 they flew in from Great Britain. (Taher Zaki Collection)

FIGHTER FLEET

Egyptian pilots who graduated from the Air Force College in 1954-1955 joined a tactical fighter force assembled during the early 1950s and dominated by British-made fighter jets.

The REAF was the first air force to fly jet fighters in the Middle East. In August 1948, it placed an order for 12 newly built Gloster Meteor F.Mk 4 fighters and six refurbished, ex-RAF T.Mk 7 two-seat conversion trainers, but – because of an arms embargo related to the Palestine War – the first of these did not reach the country until October 1949. Gloster pilot Bill Waterton then stayed in Egypt for three weeks to help train REAF pilots. The balance of 10 aircraft had been the subject of two further orders (one for three and one for seven aircraft) placed in January and October 1949 respectively. Three were delivered in January and February 1950, and others through March and May of the same year. T.Mk 7s were delivered in small batches between early 1950 and September 1955.

A pre-delivery photograph of the first Meteor T.Mk 7 prepared for Egypt, serial number 1400. (David Nicolle Collection)

The first two Meteors to reach Egypt, on 27 October 1949, were this F.Mk 4, serial number 1401 (photographed over England before delivery), and the T.Mk 7, serial number 1400. They formed the nucleus of the new No. 20 Squadron. (David Nicolle Collection)

A beautiful study of the Meteor F.Mk 4, serial number 1405, taken during delivery flight at Luqa International, Malta, in March 1950. (N. Lees photo, via David Nicolle)

Once operational, Meteors served with No. 20 Squadron, commanded by highly experienced Squadron Leader Omar Bakeer. Bakeer was a veteran of the No. 1411 Meteorological Flight during the Second World War, and then flew Spitfires during the Palestine War. His unit was considered the most combat effective within the REAF in the early 1950s, and the British assessed it as having high standards in everything except navigation and air-to-air gunnery with its F.Mk 4. Sadly, this mount proved hard to control at high speeds and in violent combat manoeuvres and, like the more numerous Vampires, also lacked ejection seats. While there was no immediate solution to the issue of manoeuvrability or the lack of ejection seats, the Air Force College set up a Navigational School at Dikhelia AB, near Alexandria, in an attempt to solve navigation-related problems. Centred around No. 4 Squadron, equipped with Beech C-45 light transports, the work of the school was badly hampered by a lack of spares and equipment. Furthermore, Bakeer was killed in an accident in 1952 and was replaced by Squadron Leader Musallam Nofall. When Nofall was reassigned to the FTU, Kamal Zaki –

another veteran of the Palestine War – took over, serving with this unit together with his youthful brother, Fuad Kamal, until receiving a much more important role (see below).

Predictably, the much improved Meteor F.Mk 8 variant was the next on the Egyptian shopping list, but the first order for 19 of the newly built jets, from October 1949, and another for five from the following December, were both embargoed. All these Meteors were built but eventually delivered to Denmark instead.

Two years later, in December 1952, London finally granted permission for deliveries of F.Mk 8s to Egypt, and the REAF promptly paid for 12 refurbished ex-RAF examples, the first four of which were delivered in February 1952 (two flown by British and two by Egyptian pilots). As a result of negotiations about the future of the Suez Canal, the remaining eight examples were again cancelled; four being sold to Brazil and four to Israel. It took until 1955 for this order to be reinstated, and another eight ex-RAF Meteor F.Mk 8s finally found their way to Egypt.

Like the F.Mk 4s, the Meteor F.Mk 8s were flown by highly

Three Meteor F.Mk 4s of the premier EAF jet fighter unit, No. 20 Squadron, proudly passing over the pyramids of Gyzeh, soon after their delivery. The aircraft in the foreground is wearing the serial number 1409, the formation leader is 1406 and the rearmost aircraft 1411. (David Nicolle Collection)

Shalabi el-Hinnawy in the cockpit of a Meteor F.Mk 8 in 1954. (Shalabi el-Hinnawy Collection)

experienced pilots, including men like Mustafa Shalabi el-Hinnawy, who was considered the leading tactician in the EAF of the 1950s. After flying Spitfires and Macchis during the Palestine War, el-Hinnawy was sent to Great Britain for a fighter attack instructor's course, and then a conversion course for Meteors. By 1955, he was serving as a fighter instructor at the FTU, training dozens of young pilots who would later rise to prominence.[6]

The backbone of the EAF's tactical strike force of the early 1950s was formed by De Havilland Vampires. Cairo expressed its interest in 12 Vampire NF.Mk 10 night fighters as early as October 1949,

but the British Government blocked any such deals. Instead, only a month later, Cairo was granted permission to acquire a single Vampire FB.Mk 5. In March 1950, the British permitted Egypt to buy 50 FB.Mk 52s, but only 20 of these were actually delivered. Left with no other option, the EAF then concluded three contracts for a total of 58 refurbished Vampires from the Italian company Aermacchi, between March 1954 and September 1955. All of these were delivered by September 1955, under the guise of deliveries to Syria.[7]

As of late 1955 and early 1956, the EAF thus still had two units equipped with Vampires – Nos. 2 and 31 Squadrons. Furthermore, the FTU at Almaza AB was equipped with a miscellany of Vampire FB.Mk 5s, FB.Mk 52s and T.Mk 55s.

Because early Egyptian attempts to acquire night-fighters had been blocked by the British arms embargo, it was only in 1955 that London finally agreed to sell six Meteor NF.Mk 13s. Equipped with a massive AI.10 radar set installed in a stretched nose, these arrived in early 1956, but only two are known to have entered service.[8] One of the pilots qualified to fly them was Tala'at Louca, from No. 31 Squadron. The Commander of this 'squadron' (actually, merely a flight) was Squadron Leader Salah ed-Din Hussein, who had completed a night-fighter course in the UK, and then taught others – including Louca and a pilot named Muttawi – in Egypt. Tala'at Louca recalled:

We became operational in nearly four months. Of course, we were already experienced on Meteor day fighters, having flown these in 1954 and 1955.

Overall, the EAF's night fighting capability remained very limited. Not only were there very few trained crews, but there was even less of the support equipment needed to maintain the complex radar system of the Meteor NF.Mk 13.

A pair of Vampires during a refuelling stop in Turkey, on their way to Egypt. The FB.Mk 52 in the foreground wore the serial number 1529. Following delivery, the same was repeated in Arabic digits, applied above the existing serial in European digits. (David Nicolle Collection)

One of the Italian-built Vampire FB.Mk 52s delivered to Egypt was that serialled 1563. Note the application of the last two digits of the serial on the cover for the front wheel bay. (David Nicolle Collection)

Pre-delivery photograph of the Vampire T.Mk 55, serial number 1577. (David Nicolle Collection)

To cover-up what was a clear breach of the British arms embargo, these two Italian-built Vampire T.Mk 55s received full markings of the Syrian Arab Air Force prior to their delivery to Egypt. The front aircraft received the serial 494, and the rear one 493. (Albert Grandolini Collection)

SHORT COOPERATION WITH THE RAF

With British forces withdrawing from the Suez Canal, London attempted to court Cairo through instructing the remaining RAF units still based in Egypt to cooperate with the EAF. So it happened that the RAF's No. 208 Squadron, equipped with Meteor FR.Mk 9s, entered cooperation with the EAF's FTU, equipped with Vampire

FB.Mk 52s and T.Mk 55s meanwhile redeployed to Fayid AB. Most of the Egyptian pilots were inexperienced novices and badly in need of air-to-air gunnery practice. Pilots of No. 208 Squadron thus towed banner targets for them. However, the condition of some Egyptian aircraft left much to be desired, as recalled by Flight Lieutenant Michael Bradley:

> After one or two bad frights from ricochets and other zero degree angle-off incidents, we were asked to send our squadron Pilot Attack Officer [PAO] down to Fayid to check their gunsight harmonisation and give them any other possible help. Legend has it that the first Vampire our chap climbed into and switched on the sight, it wound itself up its slide and fell off the top into his lap!

The PAO in question, Flight Lieutenant Chris Bushe, explained:

> I was not at all keen to show the EAF how to shoot accurately, but it was suggested by higher authority that a refusal was not in my best career interests. As we were specifically banned from making any passes at EAF aircraft, should we ever see one, we had little idea about them or how they flew. After two days of lectures at EAF Deversoir, attended by pilots from other units, we got down to the practical bit and harmonisation was high on the priority list. That was when the gunsight ended in my lap. Most amusing around the bar afterwards, but it caused me some concern about their maintenance. It also raised the point about who was in command when I flew with one of their pilots in their machines. They would not concede so, begrudgingly, I had to give way.
>
> Their flying generally was of a standard accepted as being 'average' with us. The whole thing was rather slap-dash with checklists not carried out on occasions. When one pilot, on a run-in and break, dropped the undercarriage instead of the airbrakes, I thought the Vampire would break up. That convinced me that being killed by one of them was not in my plan, and I asked to be taken off the project.

For these and similar reasons, the short-lived cooperation between the EAF and the RAF was soon over, and no similar cooperation was to be re-established for nearly 30 years.

BOMBER AND TRANSPORT FLEETS

Although permitting the export of nine Avro Lancaster B.Mk 1s and nine Halifax A.Mk 1s to Egypt in the late 1940s, Britain subsequently adopted a policy of consistently opposing Egyptian attempts to obtain an effective bomber capability. Indeed, the British were extremely upset when the REAF added guns to the turrets of aircraft delivered as 'unarmed' and officially sold for meteorological and air-sea rescue duties. While not considering them a threat, the British knew that, in Egyptian eyes, these aircraft formed a training nucleus for a future, more effective bomber force. Therefore, they refused to deliver even spare parts for these aircraft and most had to be grounded by 1953. While still consisting of at least three Lancasters and three Halifaxes that were kept in flyable condition, the EAF's bomber fleet had de-facto ceased to exist by 1955.

Despite efforts to standardise its inventory, the EAF still operated a remarkable mix of about 40 transport and support aircraft. These included about 20 Curtiss C-46 Commandos and a similar number of Douglas C-47 Dakotas operated by Nos 7 and 12 (Transport & Paratroop) Squadrons and No. 3 Squadron (Transport) respectively, and their crews were trained in close cooperation with the first

While Egyptian bombers of British origin were still operational, fighter pilots regularly trained interceptor operations. This dramatic photograph shows a Vampire flown by Shalabi el-Hinnawy 'attacking' a trio of Lancasters in 1952. (Shalabi el-Hinnawy Collection)

One of two EAF Sikorsky S.Mk 51B helicopters, here still wearing full markings of the Royal Flight, REAF. (David Nicolle Collection)

No. 7 Squadron, EAF, operated 19 or 20 C-46s for most of the early 1950s. This example, with serial number 1027, wore a camouflage pattern consisting of unknown colours. (David Nicolle Collection)

Egyptian paratroop units, established in the early 1950s.[9]

The luxuriously equipped ex-Royal Flight Dakota had been given the new serial number 113, and entered service with what was now No. 11 (Communication) Squadron, along with two ex-Royal Flight Westland-Sikorsky S.Mk 51B helicopters. Although only one of the latter was still operational, and there were just two officers qualified to fly them, the S.Mk 51 was based at Almaza and served for search and rescue purposes. Other aircraft of the former Royal Flight – including Grumman Mallards, four Dakotas and one Commando – served with the same unit.

While on paper the EAF's strength thus appeared quite formidable, in reality the air force suffered from the same weaknesses that it had for several years. The majority of commanders were inexperienced and it took them time to learn their new jobs. There were enough pilots to man all available aircraft, but they averaged only 10-20 hours of flying per month and the quality of their training varied considerably. Technical support for the air force was minimal and aircraft were flown until they become unserviceable, after which

they would often be left to languish where they had last been parked. While the runways of some air bases were lengthened in order to enable operations by jet fighters, most airfields were in need of major reconstruction and expansion. For all practical purposes, the EAF of 1955 was a force not ready to participate in any kind of armed conflict, and it is not surprising that, following the Gaza Raid, the issue of obtaining advanced arms became a priority for Cairo.

4

THE CZECH ARMS DEAL

On 6 April 1955, the Egyptian Deputy Minister of War, Hassan Ragab, contacted the Soviet ambassador in Cairo with another inquiry about arms. Solod's positive reply on 12 April was encouraging for Nasser and the RCC, but it also raised some doubts. They were concerned that once the Egyptian military was relying on Soviet arms, the Kremlin might use Egypt's need for ammunition and spares to impose its will. Furthermore, they were so worried about the negative repercussions a decision to purchase Soviet arms would have in their relations with the USA and Great Britain, that they continued discussing what to do for another full month. Eventually, Nasser and the RCC decided to press ahead carefully and slowly, and on condition of strict secrecy. A committee was formed to discuss requirements, including the Head of the Operations Branch of the Egyptian Army, Lieutenant-General Hafez Ismail; Chief-of-Staff of the Egyptian Army, Major-General Ali Sabri; the Director of the Presidential Office; and the Soviet military attaché, Colonel Nimchenko. Preliminary negotiations went on for another two months, during which Nasser continued talking with US representatives – not only about arms, but also about financing the High Dam. However, while US diplomats only gave Nasser more reasons to mistrust Washington's intentions, by mid-June 1955, Moscow became so eager to secure an arms deal with Cairo that the Central Committee of the Communist Party of the USSR authorised the sale of Mikoyan I Gurevich MiG-15 fighter jets to Egypt. In late July, a team of EAF pilots arrived in Prague to inspect the MiGs, and on 20 August, a delegation led by Ismail arrived in Prague to finalise military-related details of the deal.[1]

When the talks reached an advanced stage, the delegations agreed that – out of a common interest in not ruining their relations with Western powers – the entire operation would be run as a deal between the Czechoslovak and Egyptian governments. As soon as such details were finally sorted out, the first contract – worth £45,700,000 (or 921 million Czechoslovak koruna, of which the Soviet share consisted of 523 million) – was signed on 12 September.[2]

Slightly over two weeks later, on 27 September, after hearing rumours that US representatives were attempting to convince the Soviets to avoid getting involved in Egypt, Nasser publicly announced the 'Czech Arms Deal', stressing this was to bring arms 'for defence … not for aggression'.

While including relatively modern combat aircraft, the majority of the armament ordered by Egypt was actually old though abundant, relatively simple and cheap. Nevertheless, Nasser's announcement of the arms deal sent shockwaves around the world. To propagandists in the Western camp, this action was tantamount to handing over the Arab world to communism, or at the very least to giving the 'Reds' a foothold in the Middle East they would swiftly turn into a stranglehold. While understanding that the absorbative capacity of the Egyptian military was limited in the short term, and that it

Taken at Almazza AB after the Suez War, this photograph nicely summarises the effects of the so-called 'Czech Arms Deal' and resulting Operation 105, with delivery of Czechoslovak and Soviet-manufactured aircraft and other arms to Egypt. Clockwise, visible aircraft are an Il-28, Yak-11 (serial 524, and painted sky-blue overall), two Zlins, two Mil Mi-1 helicopters, a MiG-17F and a MiG-15bis. (David Nicolle Collection)

would take several years for Egypt to become capable of making full use of Soviet arms, London and Washington sent a number of high-ranking officials to Cairo in a vain attempt to convince Nasser to reverse his decision. Curiously, other American officials reacted with expectations that this deal might signal the start of a new era in the Middle East. Secretary of State Dulles went as far as to observe that Israel would henceforth 'have to play the part of the good neighbour to the Arabs and not seek to maintain itself by its own force and foreign backing'.[3] However, such thoughts were an absolute anathema for people like David Ben-Gurion. He reacted by advising his chief-of-staff to prepare for a war the following summer.[4]

OPERATION 105

From the Czechoslovak point of view, the 'Czech Arms Deal' was not one but two large operations – one related to Egypt (codenamed Operation 105) and the other to Syria (codenamed Operation 104). The first of the two was related to what was actually a series of five large Egyptian orders. Its original centrepiece was the delivery of 80 MiG-15bis and six MiG-15UTIs, 45 Ilyushin Il-28 light bombers, 20 Ilyushin Il-14 transports and 25 Yakovlev Yak-11 training aircraft, in addition to hundreds of tanks, thousands of different vehicles and large amounts of ammunition. While the Ilyushins were all Soviet-built, all the MiGs and Yakovlevs had been manufactured under licence in Czechoslovakia, which had originally established production of the MiG-15 at the Letov Latany factory, but then transferred this to the new Aero Vodokhody factory near Prague in 1953.[5] As far as the outside world was concerned, and even in the eyes of the EAF personnel, the aircraft that eventually arrived from the Eastern bloc were all made in Czechoslovakia.

Table 1: List of Aircraft and Armament Ordered by Egypt on 12 September 1955[61]

Aircraft or Weapon Type	
MiG-15bis*	80
MiG-15UTI*	6
Il-28	45
Il-28U	4
Yak-11	25
Il-14	20

*From Czechoslovak licence production

The number of MiG-15s and Il-28s the EAF ordered seems to have been based on a plan for the air force to establish three squadrons equipped with jet fighters and three with jet bombers. Each of the planned MiG squadrons was to receive 25 aircraft, of which 12 would be in service, four held in operational reserve, four in secondary reserve and five in storage. Similarly, each of the planned Il-28 squadrons was to have 12 operational aircraft, and three in reserve, undergoing maintenance or in storage.

The first batch of MiGs arrived in Alexandria on 1 October 1955, on board the Soviet freighter Stalingrad. They were then taken to Dikhelia AB by road, and stored pending the arrival of a Czechoslovak team tasked with assembling them. As the home of the EAF's Navigational Training Base, Dikhelia was protected by one or two flights of Meteor F.Mk 4s from No. 20 Squadron during this sensitive period. As a result, the latter unit became the first to convert to MiGs, and then served as the Fighter or Operational Conversion Unit (OCU) before part of it was reorganised as No. 1 Squadron, EAF, in which guise it operated when the Suez War broke out.

EASY CONVERSION

The Czechoslovak team of advisors who helped the EAF assemble newly arrived aircraft and convert to MiGs was commanded by Major-General Jan Reindel. It consisted of several groups of experienced pilots and various ground personnel drawn from the 1st Fighter Regiment of the Czechoslovak Air Force. The

Some of the earliest photographs of Egyptian MiG-15bis were taken clandestinely in November and December 1955, at Abu Suweir AB. Here is one example, showing a MiG that had apparently received no serial number by that time. (David Nicolle Collection)

One of eight Meteor F.Mk 4s from No. 20 Squadron, that was deployed at Dikhelia AB during delivery of the first MiGs to Egypt, was this example, serialled 1411. According to currently available information, this variant was retired from service only a few months later. (David Nicolle Collection)

One of the Czechsolovak instructors (with hat) conferring with Egyptian personnel in front of a newly delivered MiG-15bis, in Egypt in late 1955. (Miroslav Irra Collection, via Albert Grandolini)

first team – led by Major Josef Medun, and including two pilots, five technicians, two doctors, two interpreters and a cook – was deployed at Dikhelia AB, and was responsible for the assembly and test-flying of newly delivered MiGs. Another team was deployed at Abu Suweir AB (sometimes also at Kabrit) and was responsible for helping convert EAF pilots. It included three pilots (Ludovit Solar, Egon Skala and Jiri Plzak), two technicians and an interpreter. Another team of similar size was deployed at the Air Force College at Bilbeis AB.

Initially, the process of assembly and of the conversion of the first groups of Egyptians to MiGs was completed relatively smoothly. All 86 MiG-15s were in Egypt and test-flown by the end of 1955 and, contrary to what was expected by most foreign observers – perhaps even by the majority of Czechoslovak and Soviet advisors who arrived in Egypt – most of the EAF adjusted rapidly to the massive influx of new equipment. When the Egyptian Army was deployed to take over the Suez Canal Zone from withdrawing British forces in October 1955, several EAF pilots were already qualified to participate in this operation. Shalabi el-Hinnawy flew a patrol over the Canal Zone in the company of Solar, Skala and Plzak. In general, the existing experienced flying and maintenance personnel of the EAF coped remarkably well with the process of suddenly converting from British equipment, training and operational procedures to Soviet equivalents.

The first two squadrons equipped with MiG-15s – Nos 1 and 30 – were established at Almaza AB in December 1955, following conversion courses provided by Czechoslovak and Soviet advisors in Egypt, and the (rather hurried) training of ground personnel in Czechoslovakia.[7] These first two Egyptian MiG-15 units were actually more efficiently staffed than comparable Israeli units which were still in the process of converting to Ouragans and Mystères in the spring and summer of 1956.[8] What they lacked was more intensive and realistic air combat training, and a mount that was more suitable for air combats against the types it was about to

encounter. Abd el-Moneim at-Tawil recollected the MiG-15bis as follows:

It was an underpowered and rather crude, first generation jet. But it was strong and stable. While we assessed the Mystère as superior at low and medium altitude, the MiG-15's lower wing loading made it better at high altitude. The Mystère could reach supersonic speed in a shallow dive; the MiG-15 couldn't. A Mystère could out-turn a MiG, but the latter had a superior climb. Foremost, the MiG lacked power controls and high g-forces tired their pilots rather quickly. [The] Mystère's armament was much more effective: while admittedly of smaller calibre, it fired three times faster than the MiG's heavy cannon.

While the process of converting the first two fighter squadrons to MiGs proved relatively straightforward, that of building-up a new bomber-force represented a much bigger challenge. By 1955, there were no longer any Halifaxes or Lancasters operational, although the units that used to operate them – Nos. 8 and 9 Squadrons – did make efforts to bring at least some of these into operational condition for training purposes. The first Il-28 squadron thus came into being through the temporary merger of these two units under the command of Squadron Leader Kamal Zaki, who was at the same time also in charge of the Vampire-equipped No. 2 Squadron. About a dozen of their highly experienced crews were converted to Soviet-made Ilyushins under the supervision of a Soviet team led by Colonel Innokentiy Vassilievich Kuznetsov, a Second World War ace credited with 27 victories. As Kamal Zaki recalled:

I was in Egypt's first Il-28 jet bomber squadron. We were trained at Almaza and then at Cairo West. We didn't yet have a complete and operational squadron, but were able of flying coastal reconnaissance all the way from Rafah [in the Gaza Strip] to el-Alamein. I became commander of the Il-28 squadron in late 1955 and was still in change in 1956, by which time we had two bomber squadrons.

Shalabi el-Hinnawy with one of the Czechoslovak instructors during his conversion course to the MiG-15bis in November 1955. (Shalabi el-Hinnawy Collection)

Hinnawy with pilots of No. 1 Squadron and one of the Czechoslovak advisors (with cap) at Almaza in November 1955. (Shalabi el-Hinnawy Collection)

As far as is known, only two, perhaps three MiG-15s and one Il-28 had been damaged in accidents at Almaza AB by 15 January 1956, when eight MiGs made their first public appearance with a short overflight over Cairo.[9] The next day, Egyptian pilots flew their new mounts over Bilbeis AB in a formation representing the Egyptian flag for the benefit of President Nasser. On the last day of the month, the Czechoslovak ambassador to Cairo presented the president with a five-seat Mraz Sokol, while the Soviet Union provided a brand-new Il-14 VIP transport – serial number 1101 (the same serial as had been given to one of the earlier C-46 transports) – which replaced the weary Dakota (serial number 113) previously used for such purposes.

An Egyptian crew heading for their Il-28Us, coded 'I'. During the first 10 years of their service in Egypt, all bombers of this type wore big, single-letter codes instead of serial numbers. (Nour Bardai Collection)

The Il-28 coded 'K' undergoing maintenance by Egyptian crews. The EAF experienced significant problems with converting its crews to this type, due to lack of continuation training on multi-engine bombers. Training and conversion of sufficient crews to man about 40 Il-28s was completed only in 1958. (Nour Bardai Collection)

The donation of one Mraz Sokol to Egypt in summer 1956 eventually resulted in the EAF placing a significant order for this reliable basic trainer after the Suez War. This example serial number 309 was photographed several years later. (David Nicolle Collection)

PROBLEMATIC EXPANSION

Operation 105 was not yet over. On the contrary, reports about an increased flow of French arms to Israel during the winter of 1955-1956 prompted the Egyptians to negotiate five additional orders. The first of these was not related to Czechoslovakia. It included an Egyptian order for 16 warships and three submarines, and was signed in Moscow in November 1955. A supplementary contract worth 569.5 million koruna was signed in Prague in April 1956 and stipulated deliveries of five additional transport aircraft, together with a sizeable shipment of ammunition for MiG-15s and Il-28s (for details, see Table 2). Another contract between Egypt and the Soviet Union was signed in May 1956 and included delivery of 24 advanced MiG-17Fs and a sizeable batch of Mraz Sokol basic trainers. A contract valued at 36.1 million koruna signed on 15 August 1956 saw only formal Czechoslovak participation; all

deliveries actually being made by the Soviets. The last deal, worth 62 million koruna, involved Egypt and Czechoslovakia only, and resulted in the establishment of licence production of small-arms and artillery ammunition in Egypt.[10]

Table 2: List of Aircraft and Aircraft-Related Ammunition Ordered by Egypt on 10 April 1956[66]

Aircraft or Weapon Type	Number
Il-14P	5
12.7mm API-T ammunition	350,000
12.7mm API ammunition	150,000
23mm HEI-T ammunition*	750,000
23mm API ammunition*	750,000
37mm HEI-T ammunition*	150,000
37mm API ammunition*	150,000
FAB-3000 HE bomb	90
FAB-1500 HE bomb	135
FAB-500 HE bomb	1,800
FAB-250 HE bomb	3,600
FAB-250-130V HE bomb	300
OFAB-100 HE-fragmentation bomb	2,000
AO-50-100 fragmentation bomb	1,500
AO-10 fragmentation bomblet	8,640
AO-2.5SCh fragmentation bomblet	30,240
P-50 practice bomb	1,000
RBK-250 cluster bomb (for AO-10 and AO-2.5 bomblets)	1,800

*From Czechoslovak licence production

Suddenly, the availability of Soviet-made fighters and bombers allowed a massive expansion programme for the EAF. However, this phase proved much more problematic than the first one, because the years of British unwillingness to supply new arms meant that the air force could ill afford to keep many of its pilots flying on advanced jets. While the first group of pilots and ground personnel to convert to MiGs and Ilyushins were some of the most experienced Egyptian airmen, those who followed – initially the generations of 1954 and 1955 – were not so experienced. Already badly hampered by all the problems of the Air College at Bilbeis, their hurried training resulted in pilots ill-prepared for high landing speeds and the other peculiarities of Soviet-designed aircraft. Even more critical was the shortage of experienced ground personnel. This was where the Egyptians encountered a number of problems, as admitted by Wing Commander Ali Muhammad Labib, a contemporary EAF historian:

At the time of the Czech Arms Deal, Egypt possessed what was left of the 60 or so Meteor and Vampire jet fighters supplied by Britain. The EAF had sufficient pilots for these aircraft. Now, however, the urgent need for additional pilots and, of course, to train them on the new fighters, bombers and other aircraft arriving from the Soviet bloc meant that existing pilots would have to be withdrawn from front-line service to help in any training programme. Such training would also take time. This problem was aggravated by the fact that bringing new types of aircraft into operations required ground maintenance personnel as well as aircrew.[12]

Following relatively quick and flawless conversion of No. 1 and No. 30 Squadrons to MiGs, the EAF began proudly putting these on display over Cairo in early 1956. This trio was one of nine aircraft that overflew the Egyptian capital on 15 January that year, showing details of national insignia and typical EAF identification stripes on bottom wing surfaces to advantage. (Tahsin Zaki Collection)

The EAF originally acquired six MiG-15UTIs, which played a crucial role in conversion of pilots to that type. This example is seen in early 1956, taking off from Almaza AB. (Nour Bardai Collection)

Unsurprisingly, up to 15 Czechoslovak and Soviet-made aircraft had been damaged or lost in various accidents through the spring and summer of 1956, mostly caused by pilots overshooting on landing. Nor was pilot confidence helped by the early and primitive ejection seats of these MiGs; several fliers who were forced to eject having suffered broken arms. Although Egyptian and Czechoslovak technicians repaired some of the damaged jets, only 64 MiG-15bis and MiG-15UTIs remained available to three EAF operational squadrons and one OTU by October 1956.[13]

It was such problems that forced many foreign intelligence agencies into negative assessments of the status of the Egyptian military. For example, basing its report on an exchange between the Israeli ambassador to the USA, Abba Eban, and his Canadian counterpart, Arnold Heeney, an Israeli intelligence report of early 1956 claimed that, '15 MiGs have crashed in Egypt and pilots are panicking.'[14]

Obviously, in order to improve its overall condition, the EAF needed more and better trained personnel. This prompted a full-scale publicity campaign which aimed to make young Egyptians more air-minded and to increase the intake of new pilots and ground personnel. In April 1956, The Armed Forces magazine advertised, 'Fly in a MiG from Cairo to Alexandria and back!'[15]

With all these measures in force, and MiG-17s – which were declared to be a 'perfection of the ideas first seen in MiG-15s' by EAF pilots who test-flew the type in the Soviet Union – due to arrive in October 1956, Egyptian commanders expected that problems with less experienced personnel would be solved through additional training and the introduction to service of better aircraft. Thus the numbers of aircraft and pilots were thought to be of less concern for top Egyptian officers than the completely unsatisfactory status of stockpiles of spares, weapons and drop tanks. This point was also recognised by US intelligence, and was stressed in a report prepared for the Joint Chiefs of Staff of the US military in early 1956, which concluded that:

[W]ith the exception of Lebanon and Jordan, the Arab states have very weak systems of supply, transport, and evacuation, and are incapable of sustaining troops in combat for any significant length of time … [Israel's] logistics system can provide excellent support for combat troops.

Indeed, this report pointed out that Israel could sustain combat operations for 90 days, about three times as long as the Arabs were thought capable.[16]

Originally, Egyptian commanders expected the situation to improve over time as additional deliveries arrived, once all the necessary personnel completed their conversion courses and domestic production of the most important spares and ammunition could be launched. For similar reasons, they were not overly concerned about the relatively poor condition of most remaining British-built aircraft. They were looking forward to having these replaced and additional units converted to Soviet aircraft. Gabr Ali Gabr recalled what happened with the Vampires and personnel of No. 31 Squadron, to which he had been assigned:

Our squadron used to fly Italian-built Vampires. We moved to Kabrit AB when [the] British withdrew from there, and were responsible for air defence of the area. Then we were ordered to move to Kasfareet AB because the MiGs needed the longer runway of Kabrit. Our 12 Vampires were subsequently sold to Saudi Arabia [four of these were delivered in July, followed by eight in October 1956] and we were waiting to start our conversion to MiGs. When the war began, we were thus without aircraft and ordered to join the FTU at Fayid, which was flying older, British-made Vampires. This is why during the war I flew all of my sorties from Fayid AB.

Additional Vampires were subsequently donated to Jordan (see Chapter 6).

OPERATION 104

In contrast to the Egyptian-Czechoslovak arms deal, the one between Syria and Czechoslovakia almost completely escaped international attention. In April 1956, Damascus, Moscow and Prague signed a similar arms deal, and the Czechoslovakian military was ordered to launch Operation 104, related largely to the sale of 21 MiG-15bis and four MiG-15UTIs to Syria. According to Israeli intelligence, these aircraft were destined to enter service with No. 9 Squadron, Syrian Arab Air Force (SyAAF).[17] For reasons of simplicity, all were delivered to Alexandria, and then assembled and test-flown at Abu Suweir AB.

The second Syrian order comprised 20 MiG-15bis, which arrived in Egypt in October 1956. Their assembly began late that month, but seems not to have been completed before the outbreak of the Suez War.

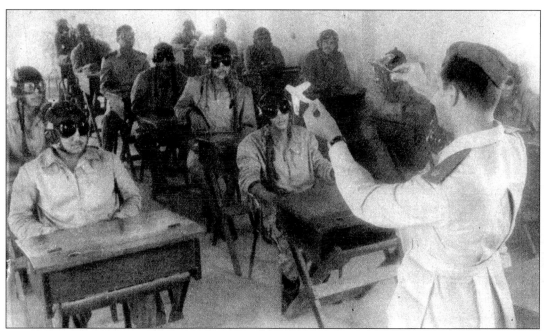

The EAF's training facilities still left much to be desired when Czechoslovak and Soviet advisors arrived in Egypt in autumn 1955. This is a scene from a conversion course for MiG-15-pilots. (Nour Bardai Collection)

The reason for deliveries of Syrian MiGs to Egypt was that, in early 1956, two groups of Syrian pilots were already undergoing training in Egypt. One consisted of novices trained at the Flying College at Bilbeis AB, while the other comprised experienced pilots who were in the process of converting to Meteor F.Mk 8s.

In order to support the Syrian conversion to MiGs, a fourth team of Czechoslovak advisors arrived in Egypt in May 1956. Also put under overall command of Major-General Jan Reindel, this included two pilots (Josef Saksun and Pavel Hladila), five technicians, a cook and an interpreter. However, once Syrian students completed their ground courses, their flying training proceeded at a slow pace. The reasons were multiple, and included language-related difficulties, but also what the Czechoslovaks described as the 'passivity' of Syrian pilots. Furthermore, the Syrians regularly refused to fly aircraft maintained by their own technicians, because these still lacked experience. Consequently, Czechoslovak technicians had to supplement their Syrian colleagues on most of the work. Finally, rising tensions and repeated Egyptian failures to provide the necessary fuel caused additional problems. The Syrians eventually managed to complete their basic training on MiGs, but were not yet combat ready when the decision was taken to transfer their first batch of 25 aircraft to Abu Suweir AB in late October 1956.[18]

In October, a group of 20 of them was sent to Poland to complete their conversion course on MiG-15s and MiG-17s, while ground crews were sent to the USSR for training. The group of about 20 Syrian pilots present in Egypt when the Suez War erupted would be sent to the USSR to complete their conversions to MiG-15s and MiG-17s.[19]

The primary effect of Operation 104 was therefore that there were not only 64 EAF MiG-15s and 12 MiG-17s in Egypt in late October 1956, but also no less but 45 Syrian MiGs, only 25 of which were assembled.

It was during post-assembly test flights of aircraft destined for Syria that the Czechoslovaks suffered their only tragic accident in Egypt. On 16 August 1956, Captain Saksun crashed while flying a MiG-15UTI (a CS.102, construction number 612792) near Dikhelia AB. A commission led by Major-General Reindl and the EAF's Air Vice Marshal Gamal Afifi concluded that Saksun suffered either thermal shock (temperatures in the cockpits often reached 40°C or more in Egypt) or disorientation caused by sun reflection off the surrounding salt marshes. His body was flown to Czechoslovakia, where he was buried on 22 August.[20]

5

TOWARDS A WAR

As Israeli preparations for a major war with Egypt were intensified through the spring of 1956, so skirmishes along the Egyptian-Israeli armistice lines continued to grow in number and intensity. This prompted the General Command of the Egyptian Army – with Nasser's permission – to expand the PBG. During that year, the 4,000-strong 87 Brigade was established, consisting of the 44th, 45th and 46th Battalions, all under the command of Egyptian officers and non-commissioned officers. While this encouraged the Egyptians to develop plans for the establishment of a full Palestinian Division to include such units, they went a step further and established a Palestinian commando force. Known as 'Fedayeen', this initially consisted of 100 men recruited and provided with sufficient military training only to help them carry out reconnaissance missions into Israel.

The air forces of both countries usually stayed on their own sides of the border, but on 21 July 1955, during UN-sponsored talks between Egyptian and Israeli military officials, four Israeli aircraft flew over Gaza City. As one of them flew lower than the rest of the formation, it was engaged by Egyptian anti-aircraft artillery (AAA) but was not hit. Six weeks later, on 29 August, two Israeli jets overflew Rafah, near the border between Egypt and the Gaza Strip, and were again engaged by Egyptian AAA. Regarding such Israeli provocations as obvious violations of the ceasefire and efforts to sabotage any kind of negotiations with Egypt, the General Command in Cairo finally granted permission for the EAF to be ordered into action should the need arise. This was the first time such an order had been given since the end of the Palestine War.

On 22 August, an Egyptian strongpoint opened fire on an Israeli patrol. The IDF reacted immediately and overran the Egyptian position, capturing 25 soldiers. Aware that a major assault was in the making, the EAF deployed two Vampires from el-Arish to reconnoitre the area on 29 August. These were promptly ambushed by a pair of Israeli Meteor F.Mk 8s and one was shot down close to

The wreckage of the EAF Vampire serial number 1584, shot down by the Israelis near Sde Boker on 12 April 1956. (Albert Grandolini Collection)

the ceasefire line, killing its pilot.

With skies clear of Egyptian interceptors, the IDF raided the Khan Yunis police station, south of Gaza, which served as a local military headquarters, on 30 August, killing 39 Egyptian troops and civilians, and injuring 16 others. No. 31 Squadron at el-Arish was ordered to retaliate by attacking Kibutz Karmiyya with four Vampires on 1 September. After completing their attack runs, two of these were intercepted by IDF/AF Meteors while flying southward at an altitude of 7,000 metres. One – serial number 1569 – was shot down by cannon fire on the first pass and fell to the ground near Karmiyya. The other – serial number 1567 – pulled hard to avoid enemy fire before diving in order to accelerate and flee the scene. However, the Egyptian aircraft was much slower than the Israeli Meteors, which soon reduced the range to 200 metres. As the Vampire turned again, this time in an easterly direction, it was hit in the cockpit and came down near the neighbouring Kibbutz Ziqim. Both EAF pilots were killed in the incident.

On 28 September, only a day after the announcement of the 'Czech Arms Deal' and in clear violation of the 1949 Armistice Agreement, the IDF occupied the DMZ of el-Auja. Although UN observers eventually managed to convince the Israelis to withdraw from this important position, the IDF then attacked the Egyptian outpost at Kuntilla, about 50km north-west of Eilat. This raid left the Egyptians with about a dozen killed, six wounded and 29 taken prisoner, in exchange for two Israelis dead and two wounded. As the IDF force withdrew, EAF Vampires attempted to attack the column, but were prevented from doing so by Israeli interceptors.[1]

Israeli aggressions thus effectively torpedoed any kind of peace efforts. In response, Nasser ordered the reform of Palestinian units and their deployment against Israel. The Egyptian Army expanded the Fedayeen into a formal unit, the 141st Battalion, and, as soon as this became operational, began deploying it not only for infiltrations into Israel, but to set up ambushes and plant mines.

Following another series of clashes through the winter and

spring, the IDF instigated a massacre by mortaring Gaza town centre on 5 April 1956; 56 civilians were killed and 103 wounded. The Egyptians unleashed the Fedayeen in retaliation, and a dozen Israelis were killed during the following days. Once again, this put the two air forces on a collision course.

On 12 April, the EAF sent a pair of Vampire FB.Mk 52s from el-Arish-based No. 31 Squadron on a reconnaissance sortie deep over Israel. The two Egyptian fighters were intercepted by a pair of newly delivered Ouragans while approaching Sde Boker (the kibbutz of which Ben-Gurion was a member). The Israelis attacked and hit one Vampire (serial number 1584) flown by Flight Lieutenant Lufti, forcing him to carry out a belly-landing near Abadat, a few kilometres south of Sde Boker. The other Vampire evaded the Israelis and retreated back into Egyptian airspace. As a result, Lufti spent nearly a year in captivity in Israel.

NATIONALIZATION OF THE SUEZ CANAL

Through the autumn and winter of 1955, negotiations relating to the Egyptian request for financial support in construction of the Aswan High Dam reached their high point, Moscow offering its help in October. However, as the detailed bargaining went on, Nasser became reluctant to pledge his economy and armed forces to a single foreign power. This was seen by Washington and London as their last chance of outmatching the Soviets. If they could outbid the aid offered by Moscow, perhaps Nasser would at least cease to be what many in the West regarded as a Communist dupe – even if the chances of him becoming a lackey of the West were considered non-existant.

In February 1956, it was announced that the World Bank would lend US $500 million to build the High Dam, provided that Britain and America lent a further $70 million and Egypt undertook to provide services and materials for the project to the value of $900 million. Alarmed that the budgetary conditions of the loan would once again put the Egyptian economy under Western control, Nasser suggested several amendments to the draft agreement. These proved unacceptable for the West. Washington and London already knew that Egypt's economy was fundamentally shaky, and that Cairo still had to pay for the 'Czech Arms Deal'. They therefore suspected that once the Aswan agreement was in force, Nasser would confess that he lacked the funds to provide the services and materials for this project, and would call upon the International Bank to finance his side of the bargain. In return, as negotiations dragged on without the parties getting any nearer a common accord, Nasser received spurious intelligence reports that the Western powers were trying to persuade the Soviet Union to join in a UN arms embargo against Egypt. Alarmed by the possibility of his only major source of arms being cut off, the president of Egypt insisted on his already stated conditions.

Eisenhower's administration was meanwhile under fierce Zionist pressure to drop the scheme entirely, and was also annoyed by the feeling of being played off against Russia by Nasser. With the president of the USA seeking a second term of office in November 1956, it was hardly advisable for him to support a vast loan to aid a country considered as veering towards the Soviet Union. When, on 19 July 1956, the Egyptian ambassador to Washington suggested to Dulles that if the West did not help, Egypt would accept Soviet backing for the High Dam, the Secretary of State quickly withdrew all US support. Only a day later, Prime Minister Eden followed suit.[2]

Nowadays such a decision might appear harsh and anything but diplomatic or cautious, but one should keep in mind that the US and British assessed that the Soviet Union was either unwilling or unable – and possibly both – to advance the money for building the High Dam. From their standpoint, they could accept no defeat in the Cold War. Furthermore, this decision was expected by many to deal a crushing blow to Nasser's prestige. It was clear that only a very tough response could save him.[3]

In the event, that is exactly what Nasser did. On 26 July, he delivered a public speech from the same balcony in Alexandria from which he had escaped assassination two years earlier. What an exultant crowd heard was something many Westerners could hardly believe. In a speech that revealed new and rather demagogic oratory skills, Nasser cemented his leadership of the Egyptian people by announcing that the Suez Canal would be nationalised, and that its £35 million annual revenue would be devoted to building the much-desired High Dam. Even before the president had finished speaking, the Egyptian Army quietly moved into the Suez Canal Zone and took over the offices and installations of the Suez Canal Company.

Nasser waving in response to cheering supporters while travelling through Port Said on 18 June 1956, following the British withdrawal from the Suez Canal Zone. (Mark Lepko Collection)

President Nasser raising the Egyptian flag over the Navy House in Port Said on 18 June 1956. (Mark Lepko Collection)

By coincidence, news of Nasser's speech arrived in London just as Eden was holding a dinner party for King Faysal of Iraq and his Prime Minister, Nuri as-Said. Said's reaction was to encourage the British Prime Minister to respond with resolution. However, he also warned about the danger of Britain allying herself with France and Israel to destroy Nasser, as that would have disastrous effects for Anglo-Arab relations.[4] Tragically, Said's prophetical warning was ignored. On the contrary, henceforth, securing the 'impudent' Egyptian president's overthrow became an obsession with Eden. The fact that he was also a physically ailing man at the time increased his restless determination to bring Nasser down.[5]

During the following days, fierce accusations about the nationalisation being illegal, as threatening the functional viability of the Suez Canal and thus the safety of European oil supplies and similar issues were published by much of the Western media. Actually, the takeover was legal, because compensation had been promised. It was effective, because the new national Suez Canal Authority soon proved that it could manage and operate the canal just as well, if not even better, than the old colonial company. Indeed, increased traffic volume in the weeks after the takeover ensured that Europe's oil lifeline remained undisturbed. But above all, the British felt humiliated.[6] Therefore, on 31 July, Eden announced that Britain was 'strengthening her forces in the eastern Mediterranean, as a precautionary measure, and that France had been given permission to station troops in Cyprus'. British commanders in the Mediterranean had also been alerted for possible military action, and the Chief-of-Staff was ordered to produce a study of the forces required to seize back the canal.[7]

Although many of the best French units were already tied down in Algeria, Paris soon followed suit and signalled its preparedness to participate in a joint military intervention. Nasser's gesture had similar effects in the USA where representatives of the Eisenhower administration signalled their sympathies with Britain and France, and a preparedness to go along with their allies. It was under these circumstances that London and Paris began preparing their military intervention in Egypt, which subsequently also involved Israel and resulted in a tripartite aggression known as Operation Kadesh and Operation Musketeer.

EGYPTIAN PLANNING

In June 1956, the last British troops withdrew from the Suez Canal Zone and the FTU of the EAF put on a large flypast – with 48 aircraft, including nine MiG-15s – over the Egyptian troops who took over the former British bases. The pace of training operations remained routine and there was no rush. Through July and August, Nasser and the RCC received their first intelligence reports about Anglo-French forces converging on Cyprus and Malta, but found it hard to believe that London would launch a military intervention in Egypt. The General Command of the Egyptian military remained preoccupied with developments along the armistice lines with Israel. Hence, in early 1956, Egyptian military intelligence obtained its first information about Israel planning for an invasion of Sinai. This prompted the General Command to deploy the newly established 1 Armoured Brigade Group (nicknamed the 'Russian Brigade' because of its newly delivered Soviet weaponry) and a number of other units on the Sinai peninsula. By August, there were about 45,000 Egyptian troops in Sinai and the Gaza Strip, organised into two infantry divisions, one infantry and one armoured brigade, two armoured regiments, two frontier regiments and a few battalions of the National Guard. Even then, the newly developed plan for combat operations against Israel remained purely defensive in nature. Its principal idea was to deploy a light, protective screen along the armistice lines, but develop a major defence line in the centre of the peninsula. The objective was to let the Israelis attack and then lure them into a killing ground of Egyptian choice. Even then, very little was done regarding the improvement of available positions. Only the old defence system in a triangle between el-Arish, Rafah and Abu Aweigla (also known as Abu Ageila) was reconstructed.[8]

The situation saw a dramatic change in September, when additional intelligence reports revealed the serious threat of an Anglo-French invasion. Concluding that the defence of the Suez Canal and Cairo should have priority, the Egyptian General Command withdrew 1 Armoured Brigade Group, 6 Infantry Brigade Group and 2nd Light Reconnaissance Regiment from Sinai, and redeployed them along the canal and in the eastern Nile Delta. With this, Egyptian Army strength deployed on the Sinai peninsula dropped to about 30,000 troops, and it became clear that the speed of any reaction to emerging threats in this area was considerably decreased.

Henceforth, the threat of an Anglo-French invasion was considered the primary threat for Egypt, and indeed an existential one for President Nasser, the RCC and their government. This in turn prompted the General Command to set in motion preparations. Top Egyptian military commanders anticipated three probabilities:
- an Anglo-French assault on the Suez Canal;
- an invasion in a north-western strategic direction, down the Alexandria-Cairo axis;
- an attack in both directions simultaneously, perhaps with a short interval between them.

The third option was declared to be the most probable, and the Egyptians expected it to develop as follows:
1) An aerial assault aimed at paralysing the EAF.
2) The invasion of Alexandria by forces from bases in Libya and Malta, with the intention of drawing Egyptian attention in this direction.
3) An airborne assault launched from Cyprus into the Canal Zone, with following reinforcements of infantry and armour from Cyprus and Jordan.

The EAF was not the only branch of the Egyptian military to receive new equipment acquired within the framework of the 'Czech Arms Deal'. The Army purchased a batch of IS-3 heavy tanks, armed with 122mm cannon. A company of these was assigned to both of its original armoured units, 1 and 2 Armoured Brigade Groups, which subsequently formed the core of the 4th Armoured Division. (Mark Lepko Collection)

Another major reinforcement for the Egyptian military came in the form of 290 T-34/85 medium tanks of Soviet origin. Most were assigned to 1 Armoured Brigade Group, earning it the nickname the 'Russian Brigade'. (Mark Lepko Collection)

4) The exploitation of bridgeheads in Alexandria and the Canal Zone to advance on Cairo.

5) Such operations might be accompanied by an Israeli attempt to occupy some forward Egyptian positions in Sinai.

Therefore, the General Command deployed available ground forces primarily in the area of Port Said, Suez, Cairo, west of Cairo and around Alexandria. Mobile forces were positioned to be able to operate in between these threatened areas. For example, the 1st Armoured Group was concentrated east of the Canal Zone, while the 2nd Armoured Group (both units were elements of the emerging 4th Armoured Division) was redeployed to the Cairo area,

where most of the strategic reserve was also concentrated.

AIR FORCE'S STRATEGY

The threat of an invasion caught the EAF midway through the expansion and conversion of those remaining units which were still equipped with British aircraft to Soviet-made combat aircraft. As entire squadrons were redeployed away from line duty and their usual bases, and experienced personnel were reassigned to other, newly emerging units, the condition of the EAF became 'fluid'. This was in turn the reason for quite contradictary intelligence estimates about the Egyptian Air Force's strength in October 1956. In general, British assessments were massively exaggerated – both in terms of the number of aircraft available (partially because of the arrival of MiGs actually destined for Syria) and in regard to supposed Egyptian incompetence. In comparison, French assessments were rather understated, although similar to those prepared by Soviet advisors who were in Egypt at the time. By contrast, US assessments and comparisons with Israel's military tended to indiscriminately bunch all the Arab militaries together, as if all of these would be one, thus paying scant attention at the fact that no unified Arab military command actually existed.

Defining the EAF as a clear underdog in any kind of a major clash with Anglo-French air power, the Egyptian General Command ordered the air force to disperse at the start of an enemy attack to safeguard its aircraft, and only later operate against priority enemy targets. Orders were therefore issued to prepare dispersal airfields for the evacuation of bases in the Canal Zone, and for pilots to prepare to fight air combats while allocating only a minor part of their effort

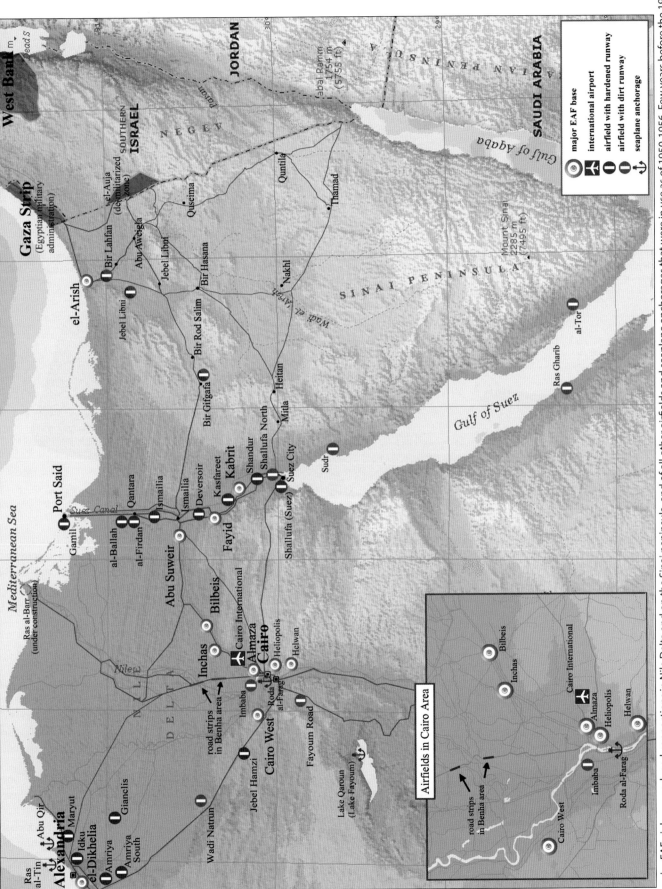

Map of major EAF air bases and road connections in Nile Delta and on the Sinai peninsula, and of all other airfields and seaplane anchorages that were in use as of 1950-1956. Few years before the 1956 War, the EAF started upgrading three dispersal airfields in Sinai – including Bir Lahfan, Jebel Libni and Bir Gifgafa – and had started laying concrete runways. Related work was still incomplete as of October 1956. (Map by Tom Cooper)

Egypt acquired up to 50, perhaps 51 de Havilland Canada Chipmunk basic trainers in the mid-1950s. All were painted in high-speed silver, but also received a yellow 'trainer band' around the rear fuselage. The last two of their serial number (1630 in this case) was usually applied on the same band. As far as is known, none carried any of typical black and white identification stripes. (Artwork by Tom Cooper)

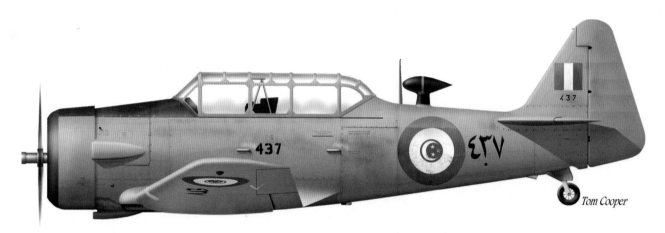

As far as is known, all the T-6/Harvards operated by the Air Force College at Bilbeis as of the 1950s were painted in yellow overall. They usually received three-digit serials applied on the fuselage side below the cockpit, sometimes repeated below the fin flash. It remains unknown if these were applied on the bottom wing surfaces. (Artwork by Tom Cooper)

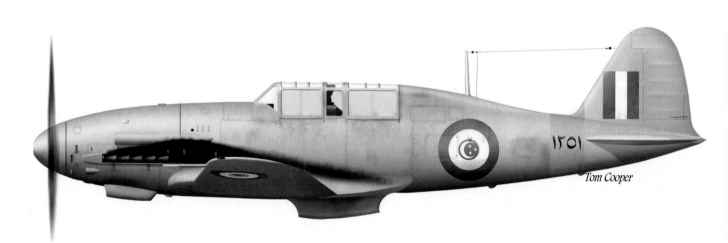

Up to 20 of Fiat G.55s and G.55Bs still in service as of 1952, were subsequently re-assigned to the Fighter Conversion Unit of the Air Force College. Some were apparently in service as of 1956, but flew no combat sorties. As far as is known, by that time all were in bare metal finish and received 'trainer yellow' bands around the rear fuselage - both of which generally showed heavy traces of wear and tear. Black serials were applied on the fuselage band, and some had the last two of the same applied on the lower wing surfaces. (Artwork by Tom Cooper)

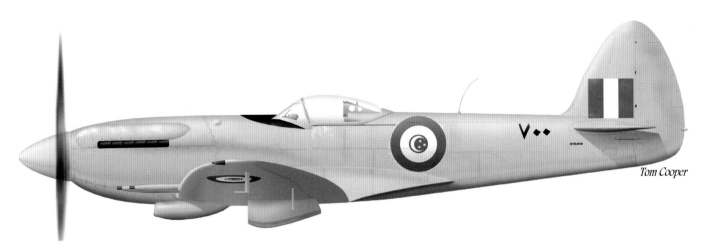

Tom Cooper

This is a reconstruction of the 19th and final Spitfire F.Mk 22 as photographed sometimes in 1954 or 1959, while already in service with the Fighter Training Unit. By that time, its high-speed silver finish was already worn out, and the serial re-applied in Arabic digits and in black. According to unconfirmed reports from Egypt, two of these might have flown a few combat sorties over Sinai on 31 October or 1 November 1956. (Artwork by Tom Cooper)

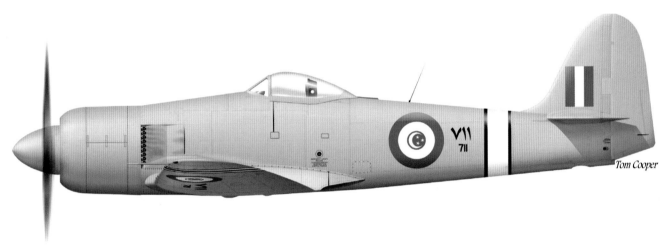

Tom Cooper

Like Spitfires, remaining Fury FB.Mk 11s of the No. 1 Squadron were also relegated to advanced training role when that unit was numberplated, pending its conversion to MiG-21s. All the aircraft of the fleet retained this look throughout their service in Egypt: high-speed silver overall, with roundels in six positions, and typical identification markings around wingtips and the rear fuselage. Notable is the application of serial number on bottom wing surfaces - in 'RAF-style'. (Artwork by Tom Cooper)

Tom Cooper

The EAF acquired 6 MiG-15UTIs within frame of the first Czech Arms Deal (i.e. Operation 105). All were left in so-called 'aluminium grey' colour which actually consisted of 5% aluminium powder mixed with clear lacquer, and was applied atop a coat of varnish. Roundels were applied in six positions, and all aircraft received wide 'walkways' along wingroots, applied in dark grey. Known serials of these early Egyptian MiG-15UTIs were 1900, 1901, 1995 (shown here), 1997, 1998, and 1999 - at least four of which are known to have survived the Suez War (1901 is nowadays on display at the EAF Museum in Almaza). (Artwork by Tom Cooper)

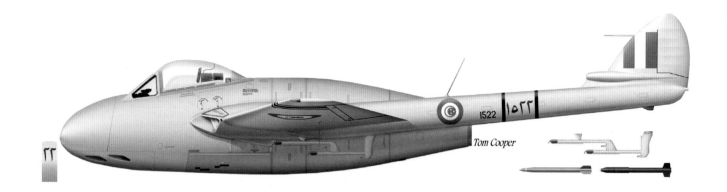

The sole Egyptian Vampire F.Mk 5 (known to have been in service as of 1956), and all 20 FB.Mk 52s acquired from Great Britain were all finished in high-speed silver overall and had the usual set of national markings and identification stripes. The last two of the serial were usually repeated on the cover for the front undercarriage bay. Most of British-built Vampires have received four double rails for Sakr rockets already since 1951. Details of these - and two types of Sakr rockets - are shown in inset. (Artwork by Tom Cooper)

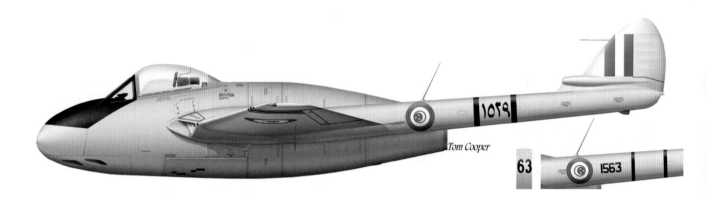

Although generally similar in appearance to British-built examples, Italian-made Meteor FB.Mk 52s received their serials in varrying fashion - probably related to the clandestine nature of their acquisition and delivery. Some have had serials applied in Arabic digits only, within the two identification stripes on the booms; others - see inset - had them applied between the national insignia and the identification stripes. The last two of the serial were sometimes - but not always - repeated on the cover of the front undercarriage bay. Most have retained their anti-glare panels applied in matt black, although these are known to have been removed before majority of survivors were donated to Jordan or sold to Saudi Arabia. (Artwork by Tom Cooper)

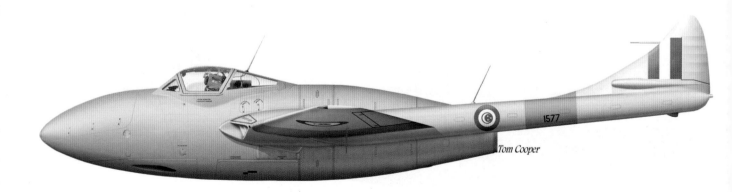

Egypt ordered a total of 12 Vampire T.Mk 55 conversion trainers, and these were delivered between July 1955 and March 1955. All were finished in high-speed silver. They received serials in range 1970 - 1981, and had yellow trainer bands applied around their booms. Contrary to single-seaters, they were equipped with Martin Baker Mk.2 ejection seats. (Artwork by Tom Cooper)

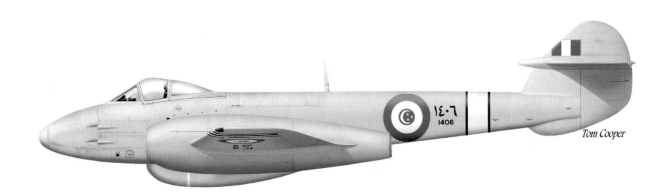

Egyptian Meteor F.Mk 4s were all painted in high-speed silver overall for entire duration of their careers with the EAF, and also received the usual set of national insignias and identification stripes. Like on Vampires, serials were applied in Arabic and European digits on the rear fuselage and undersides of wing surfaces. As of October 1956, all eight remaining F.Mk 4s were assigned to the No. 40 FTU at Fayid, but nothing is known about their participation in the Suez War. (Artwork by Tom Cooper)

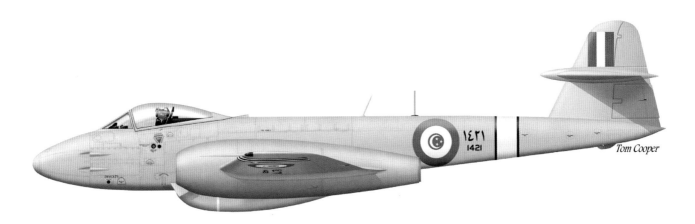

The looks of EAF's Meteor F.Mk 8s closely resembled those of Meteor F.Mk 4s. Some of F.Mk 4s and all of remaining eight F.Mk 8s have received launch rails for Sakr rockets by 1955. However, there are no photographs depicting that installation and thus it remains impossible to draw a corresponding reconstruction. Contrary to earlier claims, no F.Mk 8s were lost during the Suez War: such claims were based on Israelis finding wreckage of an example that crashed before that conflict. (Artwork by Tom Cooper)

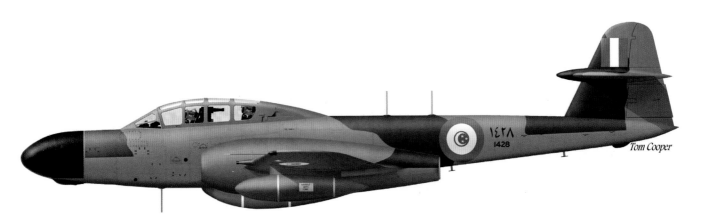

The only combat aircraft of the EAF to wear camouflage colours during the Suez Ware were five Meteor NF.Mk 13s still in service with Almaza-based No. 10 Squadron - which was actually a mere 'flight' with two operational aircraft. They were painted in medium sea grey and dark green on top surfaces and sides, and medium sea grey on bottom surfaces. While their national markings and serials were applied in usual positions, they received no identification strips, and it remains unknown if they wore any serials applied on lower wing surfaces. (Artwork by Tom Cooper)

64 out of 80 Czechoslovak-built MiG-15bis were still in service with the EAF as October 1956, and about 50% of these were operational with a total of three units at any time. All were painted in the typical mix of 5% aluminium powder and clear lacquer applied over a layer of varnish - resulting in colour locally known as 'silver grey'. Their roundels were applied in six positions, and those on the fuselage were significantly smaller than on top and bottom wing surfaces. Serials were issued randomly in range 1902-1989. Notable is that although belonging to the MiG-15bis variant, none of aircraft in question had rear-view mirrors atop the cockpit hood, and all were equipped with slipper-type drop tanks only. (Artwork by Tom Cooper)

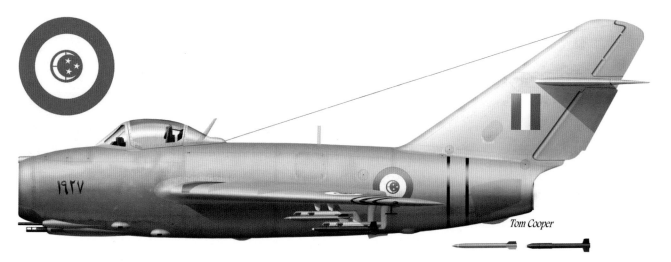

By October 1956, a number of Egyptian MiG-15bis' have received two double launch rails for Sakr rockets under their wings, as shown on this example - serial 1927 - which is known to have survived the Suez War. When used as fighter-bombers, like during some of attacks on Israelis on Heitan Defile, they carried calibre 100kg or 250kg bombs, too. Notable is that during and after the Suez War 1956, some of Egyptian pilots flew MiG-15bis' serialled in range 900-925, indicating they made use of the aircraft from the first batch destined for Syria - perhaps even that some of surviving examples from that batch were subsequently retained by Egypt. Inset is showing the way in which the roundels were applied on early Egyptian MiG-15bis'. (Artwork by Tom Cooper)

General appearance of MiG-17Fs from the first batch delivered to Egypt in October 1956 was very similar to that of MiG-15bis: they were painted in colour locally known as 'silver grey', but often described as 'bare metal overall' abroad. This actually consisted of a mix of 5% aluminium powder with clear lacquer, applied in two layers atop the varnish layer. Serials known to have been applied during the Suez War include 2004 and 2651 (the latter survived that conflict). There is a report about one aircraft supposedly serialled as 1107. Notable is that four-digit construction numbers - applied on all moving surfaces of the aircraft, but also drop tanks and pylons - were applied in red on Czechoslovak-made MiG-15s and MiG-17s, contrary to those applied on Soviet-made jets, which were always in blue. As of 1956, none of Egyptian MiG-17Fs received any launch rails for Sakr rockets: these became one of their prominent features only from mid-1960s.

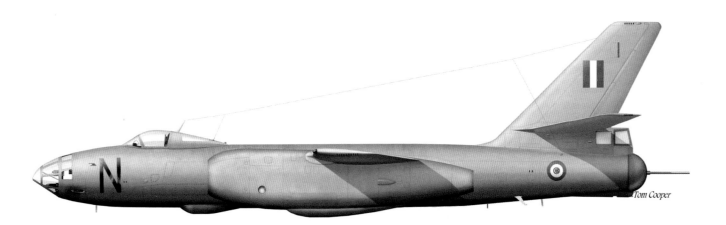

Due to lack of pilots and crews qualified to fly them, only 12 out of 45 Il-28s acquired by Egypt in late 1955 and through 1956 were operational with Nos. 8 and 9 Squadrons during the Suez War. All were left in 'natural metal overall' - i.e. painted in similar fashion like MiG-15s and MiG-17s - and wore national markings in six positions, as well as fin flashes. Notable was that roundels applied on these 12 Il-28s used by the EAF during the Suez War 1956 were positioned below the fin, instead further towards the front, like on aircraft that became operational after that war. (Artwork by Tom Cooper)

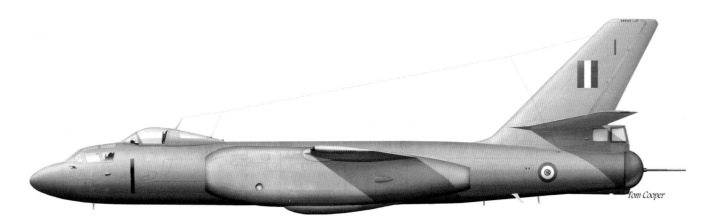

General appearance of two Il-28U conversion trainers acquired by the EAF in 1955-1956 period was similar to that of Il-28 bombers. Instead of serials, they have received alphabetic codes, apparently starting with A and going at least up to T. The two trainers appear to have been coded as 'I' and 'T'. The aircraft coded as D, G, H, M, N, O, P, and S are known to have survived the war: all were evacuated to Jeddah in Saudi Arabia. Indeed, 'N' should have continued its career at least until June 1967, by when the entire fleet received serials in range 1700-1799. (Artwork by Tom Cooper)

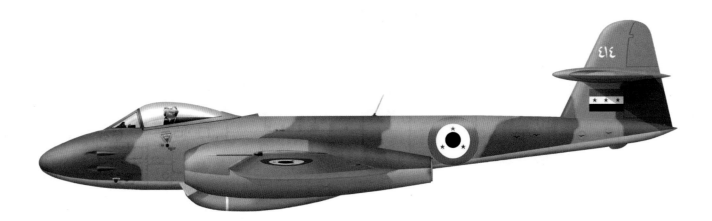

Still serving with No. 9 Squadron SyAAF as of 1956, Syrian Meteors wore the same livery as applied before delivery: a camouflage pattern consisting of light earth and dark olive green on top surfaces and sides, and sky blue on undersides. Serials were applied in white on the upper part of the fin, and usually repeated in black on drop tanks. Large roundels were worn in six positions. None of these aircraft is known to have ever received any kind of special markings. (Artwork by Tom Cooper)

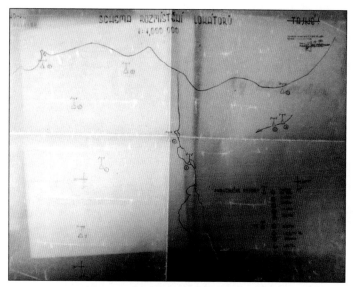

A Czechoslovak document providing a blueprint of the Egyptian network of early warning radar stations deployed before and during the Suez War. Green markings denote stations equipped with British and French systems, with blue markings for Soviet-made P-8 radar stations. (Czech National Archive, via Martin Smisek)

One of the wooden replica MiG-15s put on display at Ramses Square in Cairo in October 1957. Dozens of these excellently modelled and authentically painted decoys were deployed on all major EAF bases during the Suez War. (Tom Cooper Collection)

Four MiG-17Fs from No. 1 Squadron, EAF, underway low over the deserts of the Sinai peninsula after the war. (Nour Bardai Collection)

With most British-built bombers out of service by 1954, personnel of the Nos. 7 and 8 Squadrons, EAF lacked proficiency when they began their conversion to much more faster and agile Ilyushin Il-28 bombers, in late 1955. In turn, this resulted in a situation where most of them were not yet qualified to fly combat sorties during the Suez War. Here a rare colour photograph showing a pilot in the process of closing his cockpit prior to a training sortie. (Nour Bardai Collection)

Training of pilots from one of two EAF MiG-15-units operational as of October 1956 was more advanced than assessed by their opponents. Thanks to help provided by Czechoslovak and Soviet advisors, at least the most experienced between them were qualified of launching night-time interceptions of bombers and reconnaissance aircraft operating at high altitude. Their appearance not only scared several crews of British bombers, but caused serious concerns in London, which in turn influenced a 12-hour postponement of the first air strikes on Egyptian air bases. (Nour Bardai Collection)

Shalabi el-Hinnawy with several of his pilots and one of the first MiG-17Fs that arrived in Egypt, only days before the Suez War in 1956. (Shalabi el-Hinnawy Collection)

During the weeks prior to the outbreak of the Suez War, the EAF began adding launch rails for 78mm Sakr unguided rockets to some of its MiG-15bis. This significantly increased their firepower for ground-attacks. Two pairs of launch rails were attached under each wing, as can be seen on this example wearing UARAF markings. (Nour Bardai Collection)

The officer responsible for adding launch rails for Sakr rockets to EAF MiG-15s was Essam Khalil, who as early as 1951 introduced the same measure to a number of Meteors and Vampires. Following the Suez War, Khalil was appointed the Head of Security for Missiles and Aircraft, and the EAF subsequently continued this practice through adding similar launch rails to its MiG-17Fs. (Nour Bardai Collection)

Detail view of double rails for Sakr rockets, as installed on a MiG-17F. (Tom Cooper Collection)

in support of ground forces – at least until the main direction of enemy operations could be defined. Ground-based air defences were redeployed to cover Cairo, major air bases, communication centres and fuel depots.

According to Egyptian records, the EAF entered the Suez War with only 76 operational aircraft and a similar number in reserve. This number might appear low considering that Egypt certainly possessed nearly twice as many aircraft. However, most of the British-made jets and nearly 50 percent of the newly delivered Czechoslovak and Soviet aircraft were currently in storage. On the other hand, this number might appear high considering reports about Israeli intelligence assessments, which estimated the EAF's front-line strength at the start of the Suez War as consisting of 30 MiGs, 15 Vampires, 12 Meteors and 12 Ilyushins, with the reservation that the number of aircraft the Egyptians could put in the air at one time was even lower.[9]

From the Egyptian standpoint, much more important was the fact that during September 1956, their air force was working up for a war against an expected Anglo-French invasion and had run several exercises under the supervision of Soviet advisors. By that time, the EAF had reached a personnel strength of about 6,400, including around 440 pilots. While only about 120 of the latter were qualified to fly jets, and about 40 others considered ready for combat on older types, between 250 and 260 were currently undergoing conversion courses in Czechoslovakia and the USSR but were expected to return by the end of the year. Furthermore, the 12 MiG-17Fs from the April 1956 order arrived in Alexandria in late October, and another batch was expected for November. Quickly assembled by Czechoslovak and Soviet advisors, some of these brand-new aircraft were integrated into No. 1 Squadron and six pilots converted to them.[10]

EARLY WARNING RADAR NETWORK

At least as important as air defence exercises when it came to quickly improving the condition of the EAF in September and October 1956, was the fact that during this short period of time, Czechoslovak and Soviet advisors had helped establish an integrated early warning radar and fighter-control system. As of late 1955, Egypt had a total of 12 early warning radars and various other assorted equipment of British and French origin, although most of this was non-operational due to a lack of spares and training. Czechoslovaks and Soviets not only helped Egyptians restore some of this equipment to working condition, but also selected new equipment of Soviet origin. Amongst others, this included 16 P-8 early warning radars (known as 'Knife Rest A' in the West) with a detection range of 150km, 360 37mm M1939 anti-aircraft guns, 58 85mm M1944 air defence guns with 14 SON-4 fire-control radars, and 53 heavy anti-aircraft machine guns.[11]

As soon as this equipment was delivered, Czechoslovaks and Soviets trained Egyptian personnel, selected suitable sites and supported the deployment of the resulting system in the field. Thus came into being the Fighter Control System, commanded by Air Vice Marshal Ali Attia (freshly back from serving a tour as Air Attaché in London). By October 1956, the force under Attia's command included three radar stations deployed in the Nile Delta (at Nomman, el-Agami and Dikhelia), Cairo being covered by one (at Zamalek), with two more in the Suez Canal Zone (at Gamil and Abu'l-Sultan, west of Deversoir) and three on the Sinai peninsula. Four of these were equipped with French-made ESV2s and five with Soviet P-8 systems. As of October 1956, many of these new air defence sites and radar units were still working up, and their crews still in training, but the system was already functional.[12]

In addition to controlling the EAF's interceptors, the Fighter Control System was linked with three major groups of ground-based air defences controlled by the Egyptian Army, concentrated as follows:

- Unit 1 (Cairo Sector): 31 heavy flaks and 11 light flaks
- Unit 2 (Northern Sector): 19 heavy flaks and 14 light flaks
- Unit 3 (Eastern Sector, Suez Canal Zone): 13 heavy flaks and 9 light flaks.[13]

Although this meant that most of the Sinai peninsula remained uncovered by an Egyptian radar network and air defences, it was better than nothing. Indeed, for the first time in its history, the EAF had a relatively good coverage of the airspace over northern Egypt.

Curiously, related activity entirely escaped the attention of British and French reconnaissance aircraft which began operating close to Egyptian airspace in an attempt to discover the EAF's strength and disposition. The first such sortie, flown by an English Electric Canberra PR.Mk 7 reconnaissance-bomber of No. 58 Squadron, RAF, piloted by Flight Lieutenant G.J. Clark, surveyed the Egyptian coast from an altitude of 33,000ft on 20 October, and reported no Egyptian reaction. Eden confirmed such conclusions in his memoirs:

> For some time we had been keeping occasional and informal watch on the Canal and Egyptian troop movements. We had done this by means of Canberras flying high and often a little way out to sea. There had never been any attempted interference with these flights and we believed them to be unperceived.[14]

Eight days later, a Canberra of No. 13 Squadron initiated what became regular surveillance sorties, which included Boeing B-29 Washingtons of the highly secretive No. 192 Squadron RAF. The latter operated well outside Egyptian airspace, but were excellently equipped for electronic intelligence gathering (ELINT). They, according to Squadron Leader Wellum,

> discovered that the Egyptians shut down their air defence radars after midday each day. This was a great help when the British launched their attacks.[15]

Similar conclusions were drawn by Lieutenant-Colonel Vallet, who commanded the AdA's reconnaissance units deployed for the invasion of Egypt:

Hinnawy with two pilots from No. 1 Squadron, seen perhaps a day before the outbreak of the Suez War. All were highly satisfied with rapid conversion to brand-new MiG-17s. (Nour Bardai Collection)

There was no air support organisation [no coordinated actions of the Air Force and the Army] … The lack of a system to detect enemy aircraft and to control Egyptian fighters, and the lack of Egyptian experience in this field, meant that the EAF's effectiveness here was low, particularly at night … The EAF was most effective in the ground-attack role. The pilots of MiG-15s, Vampires and Meteors were well-trained in the use of rockets and bombs against ground targets and naval targets … About 60 percent of EAF aircraft were operational because of shortage of mechanics and this was expected to drop below 50 percent in time of war.[16]

Unsurprisingly, British intelligence's opinion of the EAF's operational efficiency was not high. On the contrary, the British concluded that there was a lack of concentration and alertness, and that the EAF was in no state to take on Israel.

In reality, the Egyptians were fully aware of these flights, but had clear instructions from President Nasser not to interfere and not to provoke the British – and also had no incentive to reveal their capabilities.

POOR CONDITION OF AIR BASES

One issue the EAF did not manage to solve on time – and indeed one of its biggest yet most often overlooked problems – was the relatively poor condition of most Egyptian air bases. Of course the air force had recently taken over many ex-RAF bases in the Suez Canal Zone, but most of these were found to be in a decrepit state. Apart from normal maintenance, they needed to be considerably upgraded to be suitable for MiG-15-operations. All had been constructed in the 1930s and 1940s, and had multiple intersecting runways, very few of which were longer than 2,000m (6,500ft). By October 1956, the EAF had carried out a great deal of work lengthening at least one runway at each air base to 3,000m (9,800ft). However, construction of additional dispersal areas, emergency runways in the form of widened taxiways, and revetments was lagging badly behind schedule. Similarly, maintenance facilities were still almost non-existent.

Under such circumstances, some air bases were used in an unusual fashion; Abu Suweir being the best example. While it was the largest EAF base in terms of available installations, and already had a 3,000m-long runway, it primarily served the purpose of storing surplus aircraft. Second in front-line importance was Kabrit, where

Five Il-28s of the EAF's first operational unit, No. 8/9 Squadron, during a flypast at Bilbeis AB in September 1956. (David Nicolle Collection)

Four Il-28s escorted by MiG-15bis passing low over Cairo in July 1956 during the annual parade in commemoration of the Egyptian Revolution. (David Nicolle Collection)

The EAF received its first 12 Yak-11s in August 1956, but the type proved very problematic to fly: no less than five were written off in a series of accidents by October of that year. All Yak-11s of the EAF were painted in light blue overall, with yellow fuselage and wing bands. (David Nicolle Collection)

A trio of Meteor F.Mk 4s over Egypt in the early 1950s. The nearest aircraft serial number 1410 survived the Suez War of 1956. (David Nicolle Collection)

the lengthening of the main runway had only been completed by October 1956.

In the Sinai peninsula, el-Arish was the only airfield with a concrete runway suitable for jet operations. Some construction work was done at a number of smaller airfields, such as el-Sur (Jebel Libni), about 25km (15 miles) west of the vital strongpoint of Abu Aweigla, at Bir Thamada, Bir Hama and Bir Gifgafa. However, none had a hardened runway in October 1956 and were thus of no use for modern aircraft.

The EAF's Order of Battle for 29 October was as provided in Table 3 above.

Table 3: EAF Order of Battle, 29 October 1956[92]

Unit	Base	Equipment	Remarks
Chief-of-Staff EAF: Air Marshal Mahmoud Sidki Mahmoud Deputy Chief-of-Staff: Air Vice Marshal Gamal Afifi Deputy Fighter Operations: Air Vice Marshal Ali Attia			
EAF Central Region, HQ at Almaza AB			
No. 1 Squadron	Almaza	18 MiG-15bis, 12 MiG-17Fs	CO Sqn Ldr Hinnawy, operational on MiGs, some aircraft at Kabrit
No. 2 Squadron	Cairo West	20 Vampire FB.Mk 52s	CO Wg Cdr Kamal Zaki; 1214 operational, some aircraft at Fayid; 15 Vampires stored at Abu Suweir
No. 3 Squadron	Almaza	11 C-47/Dakotas	Up to 8 aircraft in reserve
No. 4 Squadron	Dikhelia	7 C-45s	Acting as Navigational School; 7 aircraft in reserve
No. 7 Squadron	Almaza	20 C-46s	Additional aircraft in reserve; combined with former No. 12 Squadron
No. 8 Squadron	Inchas, Luxor	12 Il-28s	CO Wg Cdr Kamal Zaki; only four crews qualified; 2 aircraft at Cairo West, effectively combined with No. 9 Squadron; 10 aircraft stored at Luxor
No. 9 Squadron	Inchas	12 Il-28s	CO Wg Cdr Hamid Abdel-Ghafar; only four crews qualified; effectively combined with No. 8 Squadron
No. 10 Squadron	Almaza	5 Meteor NF.Mk 13s	CO Sqn Ldr Salah ad-Din Husayn; only 2 Meteors operational
No. 11 Squadron	Almaza	4 C-47/Dakotas & Il-14s, 2 Mallards, 1 S.51	
Il-28 OTU	Luxor	20 Il-28s & Il-28Us	
EAF Eastern Region, HQ Ismailia AB			
No. 5 Squadron	Fayid	8 Meteor F.Mk 8s, 1 Meteor T.Mk 7	CO Sqn Ldr Mohammed Hilmi; 17 F.Mk 4s in storage
No. 20 Squadron	Cairo West and Kabrit	12 MiG-15bis	CO Sqn Ldr Mohammed Nabil al-Masry; in the process of conversion to MiGs
No. 30 Squadron	Abu Suweir	15 MiG-15bis	CO Sqn Ldr Nazih Khalifa; operational on MiGs, some aircraft at Abu Suweir
No. 31 Squadron	el-Arish	-	CO Sqn Ldr Bahgat Hassan Hilmi; unit withdrawn from el-Arish; Vampires sold to Saudi Arabia, pilots undergoing ground course on MiG-15s and mostly served with No. 40 FTU during Suez War
No. 40 FTU	Fayid	8 Meteor F.Mk 4s, 3 Meteor T.Mk 7s, 10 Vampire FB.Mk 52s, 4 Vampire T.Mk 55s, 4 Harvards	CO Sqn Ldr Salah ad-Din Husayn
MiG OTU	Kabrit	12 MiG-15bis, 10 MiG-15UTIs	Including 20 MiG-15bis and 4 MiG-15UTIs ordered by Syria, crews still undergoing ground training
Air Force College, Bilbeis AB			
Elementary Flying School	Bilbeis	13 Gomhouriyas, 51 Chipmunks, 36 T-6/Harvards	13 Gomhouriyas, 37 Chipmunks, 19 Harvards in reserve
Advanced Flying School	Bilbeis	15 Spitfire F.Mk 22s, 8 Fury FB.Mk 11s, 20 Fiat G.55s, 7 Yak-11s	
Agricultural Flight	Bilbeis	5 BT.13s, 1 Super Cub, 22 Sokols, 22 Magisters, 2 Storchs	

SOVIET ADVISORS

The presence and activities of Czechoslovak and Soviet advisors was an issue of major concern for the British, French and Israelis during the planning for their invasion of Egypt. Based on experiences from the recent Korean War, they began considering the possibility of the Soviet Union deploying its troops, 'probably disguised as volunteers', for combat purposes in Egypt. Such a threat was taken particularly seriously by the Intelligence Branch of the IDF,

AMAN. Caught off-guard by the 'Czech Arms Deal', AMAN was keen not to experience another mishap and thus tended to provide worst case scenarios to its superiors. Unsurprisingly, the issue of Soviet 'volunteers' became a regular topic, even during meetings of the Israeli cabinet as early as October 1955, when Moshe Dayan expressed his expectation as follows:

Colonel A. Bozhenko (first from the left) was, according to Hinnawy, one of most competent and highly influential Soviet advisors in Egypt in 1956. Here he is in the company of Hinnawy (centre) shortly before the war. (Shalabi el-Hinnawy Collection)

I think that in the first stage they [the Egyptians] will use them [MiGs] with the help of foreign volunteers. There are German volunteers in Egypt and now it seems that already a group of volunteers from behind the Iron Curtain have arrived, and they are described as being Muslims living in the Eastern bloc.[18]

Based as much on exaggerated reports about the numbers of Czechoslovaks and Soviets who arrived in Egypt, and upon sheer arrogance, such reports were in reality baseless. Nevertheless, as tensions along the armistice lines increased, AMAN did intercept evidence of Nasser raising the issue of a possible deployment of Soviet 'volunteers'. Correspondingly, in March 1956, during a meeting with the Soviet ambassador to Egypt, Yevgeny Kissilev, Nasser repeatedly emphasised a request made in the names of the Saudi King and the President of Syria:

Syria and Saudi Arabia have authorised me to turn to the Soviet Union with the message that the Western powers have already permitted Israel to recruit Jewish pilots in the USA, in England, in France and in other countries. The three countries request, therefore, that Muslims from the Soviet republics in Central Asia assist them when necessary in using military technology ... Israel received a great deal of arms from Canada, France and other countries, and now the problem she faces is similar to that facing Egypt. Both countries are no longer suffering a lack of arms, but they have to be able to train their soldiers to make use of the weapons flowing to them. Israel will need three years ... Israel wants assistance to train pilots who will be able to fly the new Mystère jet aircraft ... if she [Israel] receives 100-200 pilots in the near future, the situation will change completely.[19]

A group of Soviet advisors during a dinner in Cairo in 1956. Their presence was so secret that all were issued Czechoslovak travel documents, and most Egyptian pilots who converted to MiGs with their help remain convinced that all their instructors came from Czechoslovakia. (Ahmad Sadik Collection)

Moscow replied negatively to such requests, although Nikita Khrushchev later wrote in his memoirs that 'many volunteers – not necessarily Muslims – were ready to come to the aid of attacked Egypt'.

While the story of Czechoslovak instructors in Egypt in 1955 and 1956 has since been revealed in some detail, that of their Soviet counterparts remains at best sketchy. Because the entire 'Czech Arms Deal' was officially presented as a contract between Egypt and Czechoslovakia alone, the presence of Soviet advisors in Egypt was considered so sensitive that they were always identified as Czechoslovakian citizens. This reached such a point that even today,

Table 4: EAF/REAF Serialling System, 1950-1956

Serial range	Aircraft Type
01-99	Misc. training aircraft
100-199	Transports
200-299	Unknown
300-399	C-47 & Sokol
400-437	T-6/Harvard
500-599	Lysander, Yak-11, BT-13
601-700	Spitfire
701-711	Fury FB.Mk 11
800-899	C-47
1001-1099	C-46, Il-14
1100-1199	Stirling, Halifax
1200-1299	G.55 & MC.205
1300	Unknown
1400-1499	Meteor T.Mk 7, F.Mk 4, F.Mk 8, NF.Mk 13, MiG-15UTI
1500-1599	Vampire F.Mk 5, FB.Mk 52, T.Mk 55
1600-1699	Chipmunk
1700-1788	Il-28, Il-28U (most operational aircraft wore large letter codes instead)
1801-1808	Lancaster
1900-1999	MiG-15bis, MiG-15UTI
2600-2799	MiG-15bis
2000-2983	MiG-17F

While the serial numbers applied on the majority of British- and Canadian-manufactured aircraft acquired by Egypt during the early 1950s are well-known, there is still some uncertainty over the EAF's serialling system as applied on early MiG-15s, MiG-17s and Il-28s. The origins of these can be traced back to the 1940s, when Lysanders and Spitfires received codes consisting of three-digit numbers. Seemingly, these were used as a basis for the serialling system developed subsequently, according to which a new block was assigned to the next type acquired.

This table is based on currently available photographs, while the three batches of serials applied on MiG-15s and MiG-17s are primarily based on excerpts from different pilot log books.

older EAF officers remain convinced that in 1955 and 1956 they were being trained only by Czechoslovakian personnel.

In reality, the USSR sent only a relatively small group of advisors to Egypt, and details about them remain obscure. They certainly included hand-picked pilots, many with considerable experience from the Second World War and Korean War, who proved highly influential in a significant improvement of the EAF's overall condition, especially so in September and October 1956. During the Suez War, there were almost daily rumours about the arrival of Soviet, Czechoslovak and even Chinese volunteers in Egypt, and their involvement in the fighting.

A pair of MiG-17Fs seen scrambling from Alamaza AB, in late October 1956. By that time the overall status of the EAF was significantly improved, and the air force began vigorously patrolling the skies over the Nile Delta and along the Suez Canal. Eyewitnesses from different parts of the country recall seeing several formations of four MiGs airborne every day. (Nour Bardai Collection)

However, most such reports about their involvement in the Suez War were based on little more than wishful thinking in a nation under immense pressure, and – later – on nationalist bragging. Indeed, the only confirmation for the presence of Czechoslovak or Soviet 'volunteers' within the EAF during this conflict from Egyptian or Israeli sources concerns their activity relating to the evacuation of Egyptian and Syrian aircraft to Saudi Arabia. Egyptian operational records and former pilots categorically deny that any non-Egyptian pilots took part in combat during the Suez War.[20]

6

ISRAELI INVASION

Britain and France did not have the air, sea and land forces to deal with Egypt in reaction to Nasser's nationalisation of the Suez Canal when the moment was internationally and psychologically favourable; in other words, immediately after 27 July 1956. Months were to pass as they established a joint command, redeployed their naval forces to the central and eastern Mediterranean, sent the necessary jet fighters and bombers to Cyprus and retrained parachute forces whose previous duties in Cyprus and Algeria had led to neglect of their primary role. By October, when Anglo-French intentions became obvious, international opinion was hardening against their military intervention.

TREATY OF SÈVRES

While the Egyptian government remained preoccupied with its negotiations with Western powers, it did not expect a possible retaliation from Britain and France. Instead, it was an ever more aggressive Israel that kept the Egyptians busy for most of the year, as tensions along the Arab-Israeli armistice lines continued to rise through September and October 1956. Late in the evening of 10 September, the Israelis attacked the Jordanian police station in Rahwa, south of Hebron, and two nights later the police station in Gharandal, 70km north of Eilat. About 16 Jordanians were killed in these operations, while the Israelis suffered no losses. When Fedayeen and Palestinian guerrillas killed nine Israeli civilians and seven soldiers in retaliation, a third assault on Jordan was undertaken during the night of 25/26 September, when Hossan near Bethlehem was targeted. These and subsequent attacks and counterattacks involved the IDF/AF which usually deployed between one and five Piper Cub light aircraft in support of ground operations. By

Pending conversion to MiG-15s, No. 31 Squadron was withdrawn from el-Arish AB, and its Vampires sold to Jordan and Saudi Arabia. When the Suez War broke out, its pilots were reassigned to No. 40 FTU and flew older, British-made Vampires, like these three examples seen over Cairo several years before. (David Nicolle Collection)

Five Vampire FB.Mk 52s at Amman International Airport on 25 October 1956 all former mounts of No. 31 Squadron, EAF, in the course of their donation to Jordan. The aircraft in the foreground has the serial number 1548, the second in the row 1545, while serial numbers of the other three remain unknown. (Nour Bardai Collection)

that time, Israeli P-51 Mustangs began appearing over the armistice lines with Jordan, which in turn prompted British diplomats to issue threats against Israel in the event of further military action. In another twist of fate, Great Britain was thus inching towards possible military action against a country that was soon to become an ally in the war against Egypt. Under pressure, Egypt, Jordan and Syria decided to form a military alliance and put the armed forces of all three nations under the command of the Egyptian Ministry of Defence. This decision was announced on 24 October. Only a day later, an Egyptian delegation led by Field Marshal Amer visited Amman, and officially donated seven ex-EAF Vampire FB.Mk 52s to the Royal Jordanian Air Force.[1]

Knowing that Britain and France were preparing a blow against Egypt, and with its own preparations already well underway, the Israeli government decided to strike first. Thus the idea was born to use such an operation as a justification for Anglo-French intervention. On 25 October, Britain, France and Israel signed the secret Treaty of Sèvres, which established the details of their tripartite invasion. The IDF was secretly mobilised and ordered to prepare for an invasion of Sinai, and by the evening of 29 October, Egyptian intelligence identified the mobilisation of 18 Israeli brigades, 12 of which were assigned to the Southern Command and organised into two division-sized task forces.

In the meantime, and because Ben-Gurion insisted that the French provide air cover for Israeli cities until the Egyptian Air Force was destroyed, the AdA began deploying combat aircraft to Lod International Airport (IAP). One part of the French Air Force's contingent included two squadrons equipped with 18 Mystère IVAs from the Escadron de Chasse 2 (Fighter Wing, EC), drawn from the EC.1/2 Cigones and EC.3/2 Alsace, based at Saint-Dizier. The other totalled 18 Republic F-84Fs of EC.1 (including aircraft from EC.1/1 Corse, EC.2/1 Morvan and EC.3/1 Argonne). To maintain secrecy, these units were formed into three squadrons wearing IDF/AF designations No. 199, No. 200 and No. 201. All French aircraft deployed at Lod IAP received Israeli national markings, as well as the style of identification stripes which had been agreed would be applied on all British, French and Israeli aircraft involved in the forthcoming invasion of Egypt. Their task was to patrol Israeli skies in order to prevent attacks by the EAF's Il-28s, but they were not to fly ground attacks over Sinai or Egypt until the Anglo-British intervention had started. Additional French pilots and ground personnel were subsequently deployed to Israel in French transports. They were to fly surplus Mystére IVAs of the IDF/AF, because the latter lacked sufficient of its own personnel to operate these. The IDF/AF, which had about 117 fighter and bomber aircraft, and 133 qualified pilots available as of late October 1956, was thus significantly bolstered just a few days before the war began.[2]

SINAI AND ITS DEFENDERS

The Sinai peninsula is roughly triangular in shape, bounded by the Mediterranean in the north, the ceasefire line with Israel and Gulf of Aqaba in the east, and the Suez Canal and Gulf of Suez in the west. It is an almost entirely unproductive combination of desert and mountains, divided into three main types of terrain. In the north is a broad strip of desert, as of 1956 crossed only by the coastal road from Gaza to el-Qantara. Further south is a stretch of rocky hills and dried-up wadis, crossed by a number of tracks. It was, therefore, passable in many places, but only at great cost in vehicle wear and tear.

There were few passes in the hills, and so those that did exist – like the Mitla Defile leading to Suez City – assumed great strategic significance. The boundary between the strips of sand and hills was marked by the only reasonable road, running from Abu Aweigla through Bir Gifgafa to Ismailia. South of the line between Suez and Aqaba rise the Sinai mountains, which were of no strategic interest. At the southern end of Sinai lies Sharm el-Sheikh, an Egyptian base which dominated the Strait of Tiran. This was approachable only by a good road on the western coast and a series of tracks to the east.

As of 29 October 1956, Sinai was defended by the 3rd Infantry Division (CO Colonel Anwar al-Qadi), with its 5 Infantry Brigade Group and one PBG battalion in the Rafah area, 4 Infantry Brigade and 3rd Armoured Regiment in the el-Arish area as reserve, and 6 Infantry Brigade Group deployed between Abu Aweigla and al-Qussiamah. Divisional artillery (consisting of 16 British-made 25 pdrs and a similar number of 17 pdr anti-tank guns) was distributed amongst the troops. With this, the 3rd Division effectively blocked the two main roads leading from Israel into Sinai, but was incapable of doing much more. Indeed, some important communications routes, like the road from al-Auja to the Heitan and Mitla Defiles, were defended by only minor forces. Meanwhile, there were next to no defences on the desert track connecting Eilat with Mitla. South of al-Qussiamah were only the 2nd Frontier Motorized Regiment and two battalions of the National Guard. They held a number of screening positions around al-Kuntila, Ras an-Naqb and such track junctions as Thamad and Nakhel.

The Strait of Tiran was protected by one battalion of the National Guard, one infantry company and one anti-aircraft squadron equipped with three 30mm flaks, deployed in the Sharm el-Sheikh area. Ras Nasrani was defended by the 21st Infantry Battalion, 4th Coastal Artillery Battery (with two guns) and two anti-aircraft troops with a total of eight flaks.

North-east of Sinai, the Gaza Strip was defended by the incomplete 8th (Palestinian) Infantry Division, which had 86 Brigade in the Khan Yunis Sector and 87 Brigade in Rafah. The latter was still undergoing training and was acting as a divisional reserve. The poorly equipped 26 Brigade of the Egyptian National Guard – in essence a group of local militias – defended the sector between Gaza and Dayr al-Balah.

DANGER ON THE HORIZON

During the morning hours of 29 October, two Mosquito reconnaissance fighters of the IDF/AF flew high over the Canal Zone to collect last-minute intelligence. A few hours later, a pair of Mystères was detected flying a low-level reconnaissance sortie of the Mitla Defile. Early in the afternoon, EAF radars reported intensified Israeli activity along the armistice line, followed by a third reconnaissance sortie over the Canal Zone. Because such Israeli territorial violations had happened several times before, the Egyptian authorities did not assume anything particularly sinister was brewing. Thus, there was no immediate Egyptian reaction; EAF interceptors being scrambled only when the aircraft carrying the US ambassador to Egypt strayed over a military zone east of Cairo. Led by Squadron Leader Hilmi, Ala'a Barakat thus flew his first operational sortie ever with a Meteor F.Mk 8 of No. 5 Squadron from Fayid AB. The two Egyptians obliged the US aircraft to land at their base without further problems.

In fact, it was only when a dozen Israeli Mystères appeared high above Kabrit AB, with the intention of intercepting any EAF fighters that could have taken off to intercept a formation of 16 low-flying C-47s carrying paratroopers for the Mitla raid later in the afternoon, that the Egyptians noticed anything unusual. Although visible from the ground, the Mystères were not immediately recognised

The appearance of Israeli aircraft deep over the Sinai peninsula, and even above Kabrit AB, on the western side of the Suez Canal, took the EAF by surprise and in a state of relaxed alertness. Although dozens of pilots and aircraft were available, next to none were on alert and ready for immediate take-off. (David Nicolle Collection)

as enemy aircraft because, from a distance, they looked similar to MiG-15s. Talaat Louca, who was at Kabrit that afternoon, recalls:

> Bahgat [Squadron Leader Bahgat Hassan Hilmi], was on leave in Cairo and so I was in charge of the flight. At sunset, four aircraft flew over Kabrit. Some of the pilots went out to look at those aircraft and then came into my office to ask why our squadron didn't practice flying at dusk. They thought those four aircraft were Egyptian. Then Zohair, who had been in the toilet, went outside to take a look and he shouted, 'Mystère IV! Mystère IV!' I myself was in my pyjamas lying on the bed so I went outside barefoot to take a look. I saw the aircraft bank and turn and that was when I saw the Israeli markings under their wings. Then I realised that the war had started … Then the officer in command of the base arrived and said that we were now at full war alert.[3]

The primary reason for the EAF failing to react to such Israeli operations was that during the afternoon, several P-51 Mustangs of the IDF/AF had cut vital telephone wires in Sinai, using their propellers and wingtips.

THE MITLA RAID

The Israeli attack into Sinai had been planned to permit a pause after the initial phase, in order to enable the IDF's commanders and their political masters to review the scope of the operation and, if necessary, make adjustments. The centrepiece of the opening phase was a deep raid by the 890th Paratroop Battalion against the undefended Mitla Defile. This was to be followed by the rest of 202 Paratroop Brigade advancing in a column along the central axis

The Il-14 with serial number 1101 which was shot down by an Israeli night fighter on 29 October 1956. Specially equipped as a VIP transport, it was left in bare metal overall. (David Nicolle Collection)

Field Marshal Amer and two other Egyptian officers, against the backdrop of the ill-fated Il-14 serial number 1101, at Amman IAP on 25 October 1956. (David Nicolle Collection)

to join up and reinforce the 890th Battalion. In this fashion, Israel was to confuse the Egyptians through seeming to establish a strong military presence just 30km east of the Suez Canal as part of the Treaty of Sèvres plot. It would thus offer the British and French an opportunity to issue an ultimatum and request Cairo and Tel Aviv to withdraw their forces 15km away from the strategic waterway. Since Israel would have no troops so close to the canal, and Egypt would certainly not bow to such conditions, the British and French forces would only attack the Egyptians. Subsequently, the IDF planned to destroy Palestinian forces in the Gaza Strip as well as the Egyptian Army in Sinai, and also forcibly open the Straits of Tiran.

The Mitla Defile is about 18 miles long. In Egypt, the name Mitla is commonly used only for the western side, while the eastern side is called the Heitan Defile. The latter is about 3½ miles long, only 50 yards wide at its narrowest point, and bounded on both sides by high, steep slopes. At the western end of the Heitan Defile, the pass opens into a wide area known as the Saucer, which extends for nearly 12 miles. Just west of the Saucer is the Mitla Defile, which is wider and shorter than the Heitan, flanked by towering cliffs.

Due to a navigational mistake, the Israeli paras of the 890th Battalion were dropped off their target, the eastern entrance into the Heitan Defile. Nevertheless, they established a strong defence perimeter and waited for reinforcements, namely, the rest of 202 Parachute Brigade which was travelling overland along the desert track connecting Kuntillah with Nakhl. Meanwhile, during the following night, additional transport aircraft para-dropped several vehicles, plus ammunition, food and water.

As expected, the Egyptian General Command was confused about this Israeli action. Aerial activity by the IDF/AF was detected and reported by multiple Egyptian military units. EAF radar stations reported activity of transport aircraft underway in the direction of Mitla; elements of the 2nd Frontier Regiment saw parachutes descending near the Heitan Defile, while another part of this unit reported that Israeli ground troops had crossed the armistice line and were advancing in the direction of Thamad. Finally, an Egyptian military vehicle carrying soldiers from Nakhl ran into the Israeli position near Heitan defile. Although fired upon, the driver managed to evade the Israelis and returned to Nakhl at around 2030, thus providing the first report about the Israeli presence on the ground deep inside the Sinai peninsula.

Further confusion was caused by news that contact had been lost with an EAF Il-14 underway from Damascus via Cyprus to Cairo. Piloted by Squadron Leader Mustafa Mahmud Hilmi Ismail, with Squadron Leader Kamal ad-Din Ahmad Abu l'-Rahim as co-pilot, the aircraft wore the serial number 1101 and was the example equipped as a VIP-transport, donated to Nasser by the Soviets. On 25 October, it brought a delegation led by the Egyptian Minister of War, Field Marshal Amer, to Jordan. Amer's next destination was

Damascus, but it was considered too dangerous to fly there from Amman because the Arabs feared an Israeli interception attempt. Amer and his team therefore travelled by road. On the evening of 29 October, the Il-14 flew back to Cairo, but instead of carrying Amer, there were 16 crewmembers and passengers on board, including several foreign journalists.

For years, the Egyptians refused to believe that Israel would do such a thing as shoot down this aircraft over international waters, and thus the EAF asked RAF search and rescue units in Cyprus to help look for its lost Il-14. Nothing was found, although on 30 October, an American airliner reported sighting oil patches in the area where the Il-14 had crashed.

It was only found out decades later that the Il-14 was intentionally intercepted and shot down by a single Israeli Meteor NF.MK 13 night fighter in a blatant act of state terrorism. In fact, the Israelis had intended to kill Field Marshal Amer. The lucky Amer actually left Damascus later that night in an ex-RAF Royal Flight Dakota, serial number 113, flown by Flight Lieutenant Sa'ad ad-Din Sharif, entirely unaware about the tragic fate of the Il-14.[4]

A FATEFUL MEETING

Around midnight on 29/30 October, amid a flood of reports from all over Sinai, Nasser summoned an urgent meeting of the RCC and General Command at the Joint Headquarters in Heliopolis. In the words of EAF historian Labib:

> Egypt was surprised by this attack [the Mitla raid] as it seemed to have no obvious military purpose. The weakness of the assault meant that it posed no real threat and it appeared to be pointless. As a result, the Egyptian military command was confused and unable to make any operational decision until the following morning when sufficient information was gathered.

Unaware of the plan for a tripartite invasion, Nasser, the RCC and General Command drew the wrong conclusion that Israel was acting on its own, because Britain and France had decided not to attack.[5] Correspondingly, the plan for defence against an Israeli invasion was activated, and 1 and 2 Armoured Brigade Groups were ordered to redeploy into Sinai, and, preceded by the 2nd Light Reconnaissance Regiment, to assemble between Bir Gifgafa and Bir

Rod Salem.

Amer ordered Sidki Mahmoud to recall all pilots to their operational squadrons, redeploy all MiG-15s and MiG-17s assembled at Dikhelia AB to air bases closer to Sinai and launch intensive air strikes on the Israelis at Mitla. The EAF was also to provide top cover and close air support for the 5th and 6th Infantry Battalions of 2 Infantry Brigade, which were ordered to secure the crucial defile.

However, because the Il-28s at Cairo West were not ready, the EAF launched no air strikes on Israeli paras that night. Similarly, because of Nasser's standing order for military operations not to interfere with traffic in the Suez Canal, the two battalions of 2 Brigade had to cross it using chain ferries that could only transport two vehicles every 20 minutes. Unsurprisingly, it took them between 7-9 hours to cross, which spoiled all the planning for a counterattack. It was only around 0800 on 30 October that the advance guard of the 5th Battalion reached the eastern entrance to the Heitan Defile after driving around the northern flank of the Israeli 890th Battalion. The Egyptians then deployed their mortars and subjected enemy positions to intensive fire. The 6th Battalion, which was necessary for the planned counterattack, failed to appear before the afternoon.

30 OCTOBER: INITIAL SUCCESS

While Anglo-French forces were waiting for their turn to get involved in the invasion of Egypt, the government in London ordered another round of high-altitude reconnaissance by the RAF in order to collect updates on the situation. Entirely unexpectedly, a dawn reconnaissance mission by four Canberras at altitudes between 10,000-13,000m was intercepted by Egyptian MiGs. The aircraft piloted by Flight Lieutenant B.L. Hunter, registered as WT540, was seriously damaged by a hit in the port elevator, but managed to escape. Also intercepted was the Canberra PR.Mk 7 registered as WH801, flown by Flag-Officer Jim Campbell, who saw cannon shells flash past both sides of his cockpit. Contrary to various reports since, all of the MiGs involved were flown by pilots of No. 1 Squadron, EAF. One of them was Flight-Lieutenant Sayd al-Qadi, who claimed a Canberra as damaged or shot down. Sadly, his superiors deemed el-Qadi's post-mission report untrustworthy and he was reprimanded 'for lying'. As evidence from so far released REAF, EAF and UARAF (United Arab Republic Air Force) official documents shows, the Egyptians were traditionally far more cautious in their claims than usually assessed; a fact at odds with the Israeli and Western media's persistant dismissal of 'fanciful' Egyptian claims of success in air combat. Four years later, and only after Eden

had published his memoirs, was Qadi rehabilitated, decorated and granted permission to continue his career in MiG-17Fs. The British Prime Minister said of this action:

> Despite their altitude, all four were located and intercepted and some were fired on. All returned safely to base, but one machine was damaged. This interception was a brilliant piece of work by any standard and when it was reported to me the next day it gave me grim cause for thought.

Also at dawn, four Vampires from the FTU, but led by Squadron Leader Bahgat Hassan Hilmi from No. 31 Squadron, flew a low-level reconnaissance sortie over central Sinai. Due to thick fog over the Mitla Defile, they failed to identify Israeli positions there. But after continuing about 150km east of the pass, they successfully pinpointed the advance of 202 Brigade in the Quntila area. That location was occupied by only 10 Egyptian soldiers, who quickly withdrew to Thamad, the only defended locality on the southern axis. Even so, the basic purpose of Thamad was not defence but delay, which is why the Egyptians fell further back when the Israelis attacked in full force. Reports by Vampire pilots and the defenders of Kuntila and Thamad again caught the Egyptian General Command by surprise. Only then did Egyptian generals realise the full extent of the Israeli assault. Their reaction was to order the EAF into the attack.

At 0915, as soon as the fog cleared away from the Mitla Defile, four of No. 1 Squadron's MiG-15s, led by Squadron Leader Hinnawy himself, suddenly swept in, attacking the Israelis with bombs and rocket fire. Hinnawy recalled this mission very clearly:

> On my first sortie in the 1956 War, I was sent to find the Israelis whom I had been told were to the left of a pole dating from the time of the Second World War [The Parker Memorial, which was a very prominent landmark near Sudr el-Heitan, at the eastern end of the Mitla Defile]. Nabil Kamil was my wingman. I saw nothing because the Israelis were very well camouflaged, but I didn't want to go home without using my ammunition, so I dropped my bombs anyway. In fact, it was a great success. Then I could see them so I followed up with rockets and guns. It would have been much easier if we had been trained to attack at night before the enemy had a chance to camouflage his positions.

An IDF/AF Piper L-8 Cub light aircraft was destroyed in this attack and four Israelis wounded by cannon fire.

EAF pilots running to man their MiGs, apparently at Abu Suweir AB. Note the slipper-type drop tanks and missing rear-view mirrors, both of which were characteristic for the 80 MiG-15bis acquired by Egypt within the frame of the 'Czech Arms Deal'. (Nour Bardai Collection)

Vampire FB.Mk 52s of No. 40 FTU flew a highly successful visual reconnaissance mission over Mitla and central Sinai early on 30 October 1956. (David Nicolle Collection)

Pre-war photograph of a mixed formation of Meteor F.Mk 4s (short noses) and F.Mk 8s over Cairo. Note the auxiliary tanks carried by all aircraft under the fuselage, and their black and white identification stripes applied on wingtips. (Nour Bardai Collection)

Squadron Leader el-Hinnawy in front of one of the MiGs of No. 1 Squadron. (Shalabi el-Hinnawy Collection)

Ground crews of No. 5 Squadron loading ammunition into one of eight mounts of their unit during the Suez War in 1956. (Nour Bardai Collection)

This Piper Cub (serial 47) was set on fire and destroyed on the ground by four MiG-15s of No. 1 Squadron during their attack on Israeli paratroops near Heitan Defile on the morning of 30 October 1956. (IDF)

Almost simultaneously, six other No.1 Squadron MiGs hit 202 Brigade near Thamad. The invaders' confidence was high, but the sudden appearance of six MiGs, which swept in at low altitude, caught the Israelis sprawled over a large area and had a big impact on their morale. The Egyptians bombed and strafed in pairs, making three passes each, setting six vehicles ablaze and wounding a number of troops. After treating its casualties, 202 Brigade was about to move out of Thamad when it was hit again by four MiG-15s – including

that flown by youthful Flight Officer Fuad Kamal – at around 1000.

One hour later, four Vampires from No. 2 Squadron, EAF, escorted by two MiGs, attacked the 890th Battalion at Mitla, while four Meteors hit 202 Brigade near Thamad, destroying an ammunition truck and a mortar, plus three other vehicles, and causing additional casualties. This air strike scattered the Israeli column so much that it was not before 1300 that it began to move again. As far as Israeli soldiers on the ground could see, there was no sign of their own air force. They therefore wanted to wait until nightfall before advancing again. However, their commanders insisted on pressing ahead because the paras in the Mitla Pass were in danger of being overrun.

Actually, IDF/AF Mystère fighters were airborne but remained at high altitude; their orders were not to become involved in the ground battle but only to intercept EAF fighter-bombers. Far away from their airfields, they only had the fuel to remain airborne over Mitla for about 10 minutes. Between their patrols, ground forces were devoid of cover for up to 30 minutes. Similarly, the fear of a possible EAF response to the invasion deterred IDF/AF commanders from releasing their fighter-bombers into the fray.

However, as the EAF increased its pressure with additional air strikes against paras at Heitan, near Thamad and elsewhere along the track to Eilat, the Israeli air force was finally thrown into the ground battle as well. The column of the 6th Infantry Battalion approaching Mitla from the west was subjected to repeated air strikes that caused significant losses in vehicles, even if none in personnel. EAF MiGs were airborne but failed to intercept Israeli fighter-bombers. Undeterred, Egyptian troops got out of their vehicles and continued advancing on foot, but consequently, Colonel Wageeh al-Sherbeiny, commander of 2 Infantry Brigade, was forced to delay his counterattack that was intended to destroy the 890th Para Battalion.

Further west, at the Suez Canal, the 2nd Light Reconnaissance Regiment completed its crossing via the Firdan Bridge and the Ismailia ferry at 0930, then pressed at best speed towards Bir Gifgafa. Underway there, all nine of its old M4 Sherman tanks had to stop to refuel and repair after a long drive, and thus the commander continued with only his armoured cars. 1 Armoured Brigade Group followed the 2nd Light Reconnaissance Regiment via the Firdan Bridge, while 2 Armoured Brigade Group was still underway from Cairo to the Suez Canal. It would cross only during the evening of 30 October.

Early during the afternoon, six MiG-15s and four Meteors strafed positions of the 890th Battalion on both sides of the Heitan Defile, destroying additional vehicles and plastering the Israeli camp with unguided rockets. Two Israeli Mystères appeared and were engaged by the MiGs, but neither side scored any hits.

By that time, an operational pattern had developed, according to which EAF Vampires operated against relatively close targets in the Mitla area (probably due to their greater vulnerability to combat damage), while Meteors were usually used further north and north-east. EAF MiGs, in contrast, appeared in most areas of the conflict. Indeed, around 1500 that afternoon, Squadron Leader Hinnawy and three other pilots from No. 1 Squadron were scrambled in their MiG-17s from Almaza to intercept one of several British reconnaissance aircraft underway north of Port Said:

I was in a cinema when I was summoned to meet Sidki Mahmoud at the Air Force Headquarters. He asked me if I would prefer to fly a MiG-15 or a MiG-17. I had in fact flown the EAF's first MiG-17 sortie that day and told him it made no difference to me, but that I hoped to have many pilots flying on the MIG-17, and that they would be ready to fly a mission, that afternoon. Shortly after, a British aircraft was detected over Port Said and we were scrambled. We got behind it and in range. We thought it was a Halifax. Its crew did not fire so I asked our ground control, 'Should I open fire?' I was at about 600 metres behind it. The answer was, 'Don't fire because the English have not declared war'.[6]

Unexpectedly strong EAF activity forced the Israelis to establish a system of top cover and close air support for their ground units. This proved more effective in the Thamad area than it did over Mitla, and eventually enabled 202 Brigade to resume its advance. Indeed, already unnerved by calls for help from the 890th Para Battalion, around 1500 the IDF received an erroneous intelligence report indicating that the EAF was about to launch an attack by '24 MiGs' against the paratroopers at Mitla. Not expecting such a massive Egyptian operation, the IDF/AF scrambled all available Mystères to the area. Of course, these encountered no MiGs and thus continued all the way to Kabrit AB. This caused an alert at the Egyptian air base, and four MiG-15s from No. 20 Squadron were scrambled to reinforce the standing patrol of two, prompting the Israelis to dive and attack in great haste. The first two Mystères missed their opponents but the third hit a MiG that was climbing from the runway, as recalled by Sobhi at-Tawil:

The EAF's brand-new MiG-17Fs flew their first operational sorties during the afternoon of 30 October 1956, when Squadron Leader el-Hinnawy was scrambled from Almaza to intercept a British reconnaissance aircraft underway north of Port Said. (Shalabi el-Hinnawy Collection)

El-Hinnawy preparing for a sortie in one of the EAF's MiG-17Fs. (Shalabi el-Hinnawy Collection)

Soon MiG-15s began to take off, but one of these aircraft was shot down while it was climbing. Then a clash took place between the MiGs and Israeli Mystères. During a 10-minute dogfight a Mystère was severely damaged by Flight Lieutenant Hussayn Sidki, before the Israeli formation pulled away. By some strange coincidence that was the Mystère that had shot down the MiG-15 at the start of the clash.[7]

The pilot of the downed MiG-15 ejected safely. Ali Muhammad Labib later described the situation as a 'pre-planned Egyptian trap' (which was obviously not the case), while Colonel A. Bozhenko, then still an advisor with No.1 Squadron, EAF, specified:

Four Egyptian fighters were attacked by four Mystères as they took off. These Mystères were then in turn attacked by two Egyptian fighters from the standing patrol. The situation was now as follows: six Egyptian pilots, four of whom were very inexperienced, fought eight enemy planes. Veteran fighter pilot Captain Sidqi was on the airfield at this time. He was now ordered to take off and join the combat. He bravely attacked a Mystère but the enemy aircraft avoided Sidki's fire. Both aircraft turned away and climbed. During one turn, Sidqi intercepted the enemy and fired a burst but the Mystère pilot again avoided being hit: he was clearly an experienced enemy. However, Sidki intercepted the Mystère as the enemy manoeuvred and a sharp burst of fire smashed into the Mystère's wing. The Egyptian pilot did not see where the enemy fighter fell because he was himself now attacked

Although taken during one of the parades over Cairo before the war, this photograph is illustrative of the sight that became ever more common for Israeli troops on the Sinai peninsula during 30 November 1956: a formation of EAF MiG-15bis. (Albert Grandolini Collection)

Nazih Khalifa, commander of No. 30 Squadron scored the EAF's first confirmed kill of the Suez War when downing a Piper Cub over the Thamad area during the late afternoon of 30 October 1956. This MiG-15bis construction number 243059 is shown shortly before taking off for a sortie from Abu Suweir AB, which was the primary base of that unit. (David Nicolle Collection):

by another Mystère. Sidki pulled to one side, executed a combat turn, climbed and counter-attacked but the enemy pilot broke away. The length of this combat was between 10 and 12 minutes.

While various British and Israeli sources maintain that at least one of the MiGs scrambled from Kabrit was a MiG-17, and claim that it was shot down while flown by a Soviet or Czech advisor, together with one or two other enemy jets, Egyptian operational records and former pilots deny any involvement by non-Egyptian pilots in combat during the Suez War. The only MiG-17s in Egypt at that time were those assigned to Shalabi el-Hinnawy's No. 1 Squadron, and were based at Almaza. Hinnawy is known to have undertaken the EAF's first operational MiG-17-mission on 30 October, but described it as flying 'solo', and he was certainly neither involved in the air battle over Kabrit, nor shot down during that mission. Israeli sources stress that the Mystère claimed shot down by Sidki was only damaged and returned safely to Hatzor.

Unaware of the drama over Kabrit, Squadron Leader Nazih Khalifa led a quartet of MiG-15bis from No. 30 Squadron from Kabrit to attack columns of 202 Brigade around Thamad. After completing their mission, the MiGs encountered an Israeli Piper Cub: the veteran Israeli pilot waved and bobbed for several minutes in an attempt to evade them, but was eventually shot down before the MiGs returned to their base, very low on fuel.

Regarding the Israeli appearance over Kabrit AB as an attempted attack and a provocation, during the evening of 30 October, the EAF ordered attacks on Israeli air bases by Il-28 bombers of the combined Nos 8/9 Squadron, despite their crews still lacking experience in operating these twin-engined jet bombers. Two Il-28s each were launched to attack the airfields at Hatzor and Tel Nov, and – according to several former Egyptian pilots – they bombed air bases known to EAF as Qastina (Hatzor), Aqir (Tel Nov) and Ramat David. Their crews reported causing large fires,[8] but according to Israeli sources, just one stick of bombs released by one bomber fell somewhere in the Ramat Razi'el area, east of Jerusalem, while the other attacks were entirely ineffective.

Nevertheless, the Egyptians – and particularly the EAF – looked back at this first day of serious fighting with considerable satisfaction. The EAF had launched over 50 combat sorties, losing only one MiG-15 in the process. Because most of the pilots lacked skills and realistic training to take full advantage of their new mounts, their commanders emphasised organisation and safety over

aggressiveness. Correspondingly, most EAF fighter-bombers flew disruptive air strikes against ground targets. They pinned down the 890th Battalion near Heitan Defile, thus exposing it to constant pressure from the 5th Infantry Battalion. The Egyptians were also convinced that, were it not for the late arrival of the 6th Infantry Battalion, Israeli troops east of Mitla would have been overrun. While they did not dispute that the rest of 202 Paratrooper Brigade made significant advances from Quntila via Thamad, they knew this was then delayed by air strikes which destroyed at least 23 Israeli vehicles. In the course of related operations, EAF pilots claimed an Israeli Mystère and a Piper Cub as shot down in air combats, and destroyed another Piper Cub on the ground, while Egyptian ground defences claimed an Israeli Meteor, two Mustangs and several Mosquitoes.

Elsewhere on the Sinai peninsula, the first Israeli assault on Abu Aweigla was thrown back in confusion. While the seriousness of the Israeli invasion could no longer be disputed, and Egyptian ground troops deployed in this part of Sinai were unable to do more than hold their positions, they had at least managed to secure the critical area. With this, they bought plenty of time for 1 and 2 Armoured Brigade Groups to set up their killing field between Bir Gifgafa and Bir Rod Salim. Overall, the situation was therefore stable.

ANGLO-FRENCH ULTIMATUM

It was at this moment, at 1900 Cairo Time, that Britain and France issued an ultimatum for both sides to evacuate an area 16km (10 miles) to either side of the Suez Canal. While the Egyptians promptly rejected the ultimatum, it was only now that Nasser, the RCC and General Command realised that they were facing an invasion by three countries, not just by Israel. The question was what to do. This resulted in a major argument between Nasser and Amer. The president wanted to withdraw all armour from Sinai to defend the Suez Canal Zone, while Amer wanted to continue what had so far been a successful fight against the Israelis in the peninsula. Nasser won through a political rather than military argument, concluding that the entire purpose of any invasion was to occupy the Suez Canal Zone. So he insisted that all available reserves be sent to Port Said and Ismailia.

An order was therefore issued for all reserves to be sent to Port Said and Ismailia. However, it seems that Amer did whatever was possible to delay the withdrawal from Sinai, and for most of 31 October, 1 and 2 Armoured Brigade Groups continued moving towards the Bir Gifgafa and Bir Rod Salim area.

Nasser also wanted the EAF to avoid fighting the highly experienced and well-equipped air forces of two Western European powers, whereas Amer wanted the EAF to fight everybody. In

Shalabi el-Hinnawy exiting the cockpit of a MiG-17F after the Suez War. As commander of No. 1 Squadron, EAF, he played an important role not only in the course of conversion of his unit to Czechoslovak and Soviet-made aircraft, but also in defence against Israeli aggression during the first two days of the Suez War. (Shalabi el-Hinnawy Collection)

Although their crews were still not fully prepared for combat, commanders of Nos 8 and 9 Squadrons, EAF, were eager to get involved in combat at the earliest possible opportunity. Here, their crews are about to board Il-28s coded 'N' and 'K'. (Nour Bardai Collection)

attempt to compensate for a lack of qualified pilots and increase the EAF's sortie rate, the Egyptian Minister of War issued two orders. All new MiG-15 pilots judged to have completed enough of their conversion courses to be sent into combat were to join operational units, along with whatever MiGs were available. The ground crews of each squadron were to get multiple aircraft prepared and available for each pilot. In that way, after a pilot returned from one mission, he could immediately jump into another fuelled and armed aircraft and take off for a further sortie.

Ultimately, Nasser also won this argument and the EAF was

ordered to start dispersing its combat aircraft. Twenty MiG-15s were redeployed from the Suez Canal Zone to dispersal airfields set up in the Nile Delta early on 31 October. Meanwhile, Czechoslovak and Soviet advisors flew all aircraft for which there were not enough Egyptian crews via Luxor to Saudi Arabia and Syria. The first to go were at least nine Il-28s and one Il-14 transport.

Of course, the commanders of various EAF units did not run away, but began preparing defences against an Anglo-French onslaught, while continuing their operations against the Israelis. Shalabi el-Hinnawy described his actions from the morning of 31 October as follows:

> When the 1956 War started, I told my superiors that I thought it would be a short war but that we should disperse our aircraft. They didn't issue such an order to me, but my squadron did disperse its MiGs. The only exceptions were the four or six aircraft we were actually using. We took the others from the operational area of Almaza to the scrap area of this air base. There we covered them in old tyres and pieces of corrugated iron so that they would be unseen. There were 22 of these aircraft there and not one of them ever got hit.

Next, Hinnawy met Kamal Zaki, the CO of the combined Il-28-squadrons:

> Kamal Zaki wanted to attack Israeli troops in the Beersheba area, flying from Almaza. He prepared six Il-28s and asked me to provide top cover with 12 MiG-15s and MiG-17s. When I calculated the route, it turned out it would have been impossible for the MiGs to get back to Almaza. They lacked the necessary range. Therefore, this mission was cancelled.

31 OCTOBER: ALL-OUT EFFORT

By the time the Anglo-French ultimatum expired at 0600 on 31 October, the pilots of No. 1 Squadron sat in their cockpits waiting for the British and French bombers to appear. However, the only activity which Egyptian early warning radars detected that morning over the Nile Delta and Suez Canal Zone was a total of 11 reconnaissance sorties by RAF Canberras and AdA RF-84Fs. The EAF scrambled several MiGs to intercept and two of these caught a solitary French reconnaissance fighter. The pilot of the latter never noticed his opponents but, upon seeing tracers wizzing past his cockpit, immediately aborted his mission and returned to Cyprus. Photographs brought back by other aircraft prompted the British to conclude that the EAF had over 110 operational MiG-15s, 14 Meteors, 44 Vampires and 48 Il-28 bombers, deployed as follows:

- Cairo West: nine Vampires, 16 Il-28s
- Almaza: 25 MiG-15/17, four Meteors, 21 Vampires, 10 Il-28s
- Inchas: 20 MiG-15s
- Abu Suweir: 35 MiG-15s
- Kabrit: 31 MiG-15s
- Fayd: nine Meteors, 12 Vampires
- Kasfareet: one Meteor, two Vampires
- Luxor: 22 Il-28s.

This suggested that the EAF would prove far more dangerous than had been expected, and, fearing an interception of their bombers by MiGs, the Anglo-French commanders decided to postpone their air strikes until the following evening. This delay in turn enabled the Czechoslovaks and Soviets to evacuate their personnel and a considerable amount of aircraft and material from major EAF air bases. Indeed, by noon, all but eight Il-28s of the combined Nos 8/9

A pre-war photograph of three EAF Vampire FB.Mk 52s. Notable are typical national- and identification markings, but also four rails for Sakr rockets installed on each of the aircraft. (Albert Grandolini Collection)

Three EAF Vampires underway low over the Nile River before the war. The type's vulnerability and obsolescence was fully exposed on the morning of 31 October 1956, when three fighters of No. 40 FTU were shot down by two Israeli Mystères within a few minutes over the Mitla Defile. (David Nicolle Collection)

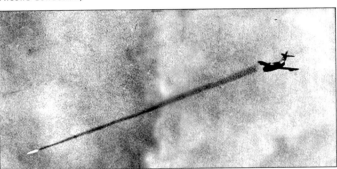

A retouched photograph showing one of the MiG-15bis modified to carry Sakr rockets demonstrating their deployment. The addition of a launch rail for unguided rockets significantly bolstered the firepower of this type. (Nour Bardai Collection)

Squadron had either been flown to Luxor airfield or were already outside the country. They were followed by 10 Egyptian MiG-15s from reserve, and at least three, possibly all four, MiG-15UTIs destined for the SyAAF. Furthermore, most combat aircraft assigned to units of the EAF's Central Region were dispersed.

Meanwhile, during the night of 30/31 October, the Egyptian General Command received reports that 202 Paratroop Brigade had managed to reach and reinforce Israelis east of the Heitan Defile. Therefore, it rushed in reinforcements of mortars and flak to 2 Brigade and ordered this unit to dig in and defend its positions. Correspondingly, the EAF Eastern Region launched an all-out effort against Israeli units. In an attempt to hit Israeli paras before any IDF/AF combat air patrols would arrive over the area, the FTU at Fayid launched a rushed attack on Mitla, without properly coordinating this mission with MiG-squadrons at Kabrit. Talat Louca recalled a fateful decision taken minutes before take-off:

Bahgat Hilmi was on the First Stage Alert, and I was on the Second. It was my turn to fly, but on my way to the briefing, Bahgat said it was his, and he went to the briefing instead.

Thus, four Vampire FB.Mk 52s – led by Squadron Leader Hilmi and piloted by Pilot Officer Mahmmoud Wael Afifi, Flight Officer Ahmad Farghal and Pilot Officer Gabr Ali Gabr – approached Mitla without any top cover. Gabr Ali Gabr recalled what happened when his formation was bounced by two Mystères:

We pressed our attack despite morning mist, each making one pass. I noticed we were under attack only when Bahgat, Afifi and Farghal were hit and caught fire. I flew some horizontal evasion manoeuvres because in this respect the Vampire was superior to the Mystère. My aircraft still had all of its eight rockets attached. As I was looking for my colleagues, I saw a Mystère right in front of me: it was turning left and was at about maximum firing range, so I tried a burst. The Mystère abruptly turned right, dove and disappeared.

Then I saw the Vampire either flown by Bahgat or Farghal spinning and on fire. There was no parachute. I saw another Vampire, flown by Afifi, flying west and with fire coming out of the flaps area. I approached to about 50m of his wing, and could see the pilot clearly, but his head was not moving: he was either wounded or dead. Fearing his Vampire would explode, I moved a bit further away. The aircraft then fell and crashed.

I contacted our tower, where Ahmad Nassr was on duty, and was told to land at Kabrit because of morning mist. When I landed at Kabrit, I was furious and overexcited. I went straight to the base commander and demanded to know why the MiGs had not been there to give us cover. The commander whose name I think was Hassan Abou Zaid [not related to other officers named Abou Zaid in the EAF], could not answer and shrugged his shoulders. The official explanation that emerged later was, 'due to mist'. But,

the Vampire mission was not aborted due to fog and we pressed ahead without cover …?

Later on I was debriefed and Bahig Hamza, my former instructor, reviewed my gun-camera film. He said that my burst of cannon fire undershot the target, and there was only a distant chance I might have caused some damage.[9]

An hour later, a quartet of MiG-17s from Almaza arrived over Mitla and engaged a pair of Israeli fighters, in turn prompting EAF historian Labib to explain:

The Mystères then fell into a trap [from] this MiG air cover and as a result high losses were inflicted upon them, despite the fact that [the] MiG-17 pilots had only been flying their jets for [a] short time.'

This claim was not borne out by the facts. The two Israeli aircraft engaged by MiG-17Fs from No.1 Squadron were actually Meteors and neither was shot down. Nevertheless, the IDF/AF did suffer heavy losses that morning during attacks on the Abu Aweigla stronghold. Here, Egyptian Army units showed excellent aiming skills and shot down at least one P-51, two Mosquitoes and two out of four Harvards which attempted to dive-bomb them.

Down on the ground, after having failed to achieve his objective of securing Mitla, and realising the exposed position of his troops in the open desert east of the Heitan Defile, the commander of 202 Paratroop Brigade decided to advance into the pass. Dayan forbade the attack, but agreed to a reconnaissance. Correspondingly, two companies of paras mounted in half-tracks and the brigade reconnaissance unit travelling in trucks, supported by three AMX-13 light tanks, one battery of 120mm mortars and one of 25 pdr field guns, passed by the Parker Monument, east of the Heitan Defile, and drove into the winding pass at around noon. Once there, the Israeli convoy came under intense fire from three sides, which left two half-tracks and one tank disabled, and troops scattered amongst the boulders on the floor of the pass. The second Israeli column

According to unconfirmed reports from Egypt, EAF Furies might have flown several combat sorties on 31 October 1956. This Fury, serial number 711, is seen before the war. (David Nicolle Collection)

A poor quality but highly interesting close-up photograph of an EAF Vampire, apparently taken shortly before the Suez War showing launch rails for Sakr rockets installed by Essam Khallil under its wing. One of these fighters scored the second confirmed kill by the EAF, downing an IDF/AF Mustang piston-engined fighter over Sinai on 31 October 1956. (Nour Bardai Collection)

followed, but lost a fuel and an ammunition truck, plus three other vehicles, all of which went up on flames. Amid the confusion, part of the Israeli unit dashed for the 'Saucer', or Wadi al-Hag, leaving another half-track, one tank, a jeep and an ambulance destroyed as it went. For seven hours, from 1300 until 2000, the Israeli paras remained pinned down, suffering heavy casualties all the time from additional Egyptian air strikes.

However, troops of 2 Infantry Brigade failed to exploit their advantageous position. Eventually, they left alone and exposed the 4th Company of the 5th Battalion. This was hit in the flank by the Israeli reconnaissance company and overwhelmed. Even then, it was only after nightfall and in fierce hand-to-hand fighting that the Israelis were able to climb the cliffs and force the Egyptians out of one position after the other. By 2000, resistance had ceased, the 4th Company having fought fiercely to the last bullet and the last man. At least 38 Israelis and nearly 200 Egyptian troops were killed for what was actually no Israeli gain at all. Not only was the Mitla Defile still under Egyptian control, but the exhausted paras subsequently withdrew to the east of Heitan; for the rest of the Suez War, the Israelis tended to avoid the area altogether.

Elsewhere during the morning of 31 October, the focus of aerial actions by both sides switched to the central axis, where 1 Armoured Brigade Group reached Bir Gifgafa and then continued its march in the direction of Jebel Libni, apparently in an attempt to reinforce the defenders of Abu Aweigla, who were in the process of being surrounded by the Israelis. The EAF scrambled multiple formations of MiGs and Vampires from Kabrit and Abu Suweir to provide air cover and the sky quickly filled with jet fighters that became involved in a series of confusing air battles.

As far as can be reconstructed from several different accounts so far available from Egyptian sources, the first of these involved eight MiG-15bis from Kabrit that flew top cover for four Meteors from No. 5 Squadron and four Vampires from No. 31 Squadron. The Meteors and Vampires were to strike Israeli ground troops in the Jebel Libni area. Underway from Bir Hama in the direction of Jebel Libni, one section of the MiG formation was distracted by a pair of Ouragans, as recalled by Colonel Bozhenko:

Four fighters, commanded by Squadron Leader Abd el-Aziz [real name Nazih] Khalifa, flew to Sinai. After making an attack on an Israeli column in central Sinai, the Egyptian pilots saw a pair of Ouragans approaching. Khalifa decided to divide into pairs and enter a dogfight. He gave his orders and within a moment, the aircraft re-formed: Squadron Leader Khalifa and Flight Officer Kefi formed the first pair, Flight Lieutenant Badr and Flight Officer Zein the second. The Khalifa-Kefi pair took on the enemy leader, while [the] Badr-Zein pair took on the Israeli wingman. Both Ouragans jettisoned their drop tanks and

started to manoeuvre. Khalifa intercepted the enemy on his next manoeuvre and opened fire from a range of 150m. He hit the Ouragan's wing and the enemy fighter fell. Badr and Zein then attacked the second Ouragan, which exploded in the air a few seconds later.[10]

Ala'a Barakat, who flew as Number 4 during his first combat sortie of this war, described the sight in front of him:

Our MiGs engaged two Israelis. One broke away and disengaged, while the second – unable to release one of its drop tanks – went into a spin. Consequently, we thought we had shot it down.

According to Israeli sources, only one Ouragan was hit during this air combat, before a pair of Mystères returning from a patrol over Mitla helped extract the slower fighter-bombers. One of the Mystères subsequently run out of fuel while returning to Hatzor, the pilot making a soft belly landing and his aircraft subsequently being repaired. On the way back from that mission, the rearmost part of the Egyptian formation bounced a pair of Mustangs that were returning from an attack on a column of 1 Armoured Brigade Group somewhere between Bir Gifgafa and Bir Hama. The Egyptians stress that Flight Lieutenant Zuhayr hit one of the Mustangs, forcing it to crash-land in the desert. Israeli sources confirmed such a loss, but credited it to air defences of 1 Armoured Brigade Group.[11]

Around 1300, one formation of MiG-15s intercepted another pair of Ouragans, and claimed one probable, but it seems that neither of the two Israeli jets was hit. Only minutes later, four MiG-15s that had taken off from Abu Suweir clashed with a pair of Ouragans between Bir Hama and Bir Hasana. A five-minute chaotic dogfight ensued in which most of the Egyptians concentrated on attacking one of the Israelis, while Farouq el-Ghazzawi fought alone against the other:

We were briefed to fly with two sections of two in an open battle formation and to patrol over Sinai at 6,000m (almost 20,000ft). I picked up a target, which was flying low on a reverse course heading south-west. I told my squadron-mates about the target and they said, 'You lead and we will follow.' It was my first engagement with an enemy aircraft so I should have checked whether my leader was following me or not but all I remember was how excited I was. I kept my eye on the enemy aircraft, started to close and prepared the guns. Then I discovered that I was not alone but

I kept my gunsight on the plane and fired one, two, three bursts. He was from time to time changing direction to throw off my aim. All of a sudden I heard two booms, then nothing. I thought it was a bump from flying through his slipstream. My target reversed his steep turn and then I felt a severe crash and I was at a high angle of attack, perhaps 40°, and the stick was jammed. I put on full throttle, there was no afterburner in the MiG-15, and I climbed to 6,000m and found myself alone. It was calm, not a word on the radio. I had taken a bullet through the canopy so I was losing pressurisation but luckily I could fly straight and level. I moved the stick and it jammed in a slight upward position. I came close to the Suez Canal and I was still losing height and was worried because there was a big hole in the wing. I was worried that the enemy fire had damaged the undercarriage. But, luckily, I came in and landed OK. In the debrief, we figured out what had happened: I surprised and hit an Israeli Ouragan, and his number two came in and attacked me. Later I found out that the plane I hit had to crash-land.[12]

Ghazzawi claimed a victory over one Ouragan and the EAF credited him with a probable, but the Israelis deny having suffered any such losses. Fuad Kamal found himself up against Israeli fighters only a few hours later: at around 1300, one flight of MiG-15s from Abu Suweir AB and Kabrit were each sent to attack Israeli troops in the Abu Aweigla area; MiGs from the former air base were providing top cover for those from the latter. Due north of Bir Hasana, the Egyptians ran into two pairs of Mystères, as recalled by Kamal:

We had taken off from Kabrit and were on a mission to help an army unit that was almost surrounded. Ten MiGs had taken off, four to do the ground attack and six to cover them. I was part of the air cover and was the most junior pilot. Thus, I was placed on the outside of the formation of four plus two aircraft. I was in the most exposed position and my job was to keep a lookout.

I saw the enemy formation turning in behind us and called on the radio, 'Enemy aircraft, enemy aircraft! Bandits at four o'clock!' They were at the same level as us but nobody reacted, as if no one had heard. I looked again and saw a row of bullets approaching me. My aircraft was hit and under my feet I could feel a shock. The aircraft shook violently, the cockpit filled with smoke and the MiG started to spin. The ejection seat gave no protection to the face and had to be triggered from the arm-rest. I had to pull back my feet from the pedals and to eject the cockpit canopy manually, by lifting the front: then the airstream ripped it away. By the time I ejected, the aircraft was totally on fire and it blew up immediately after I was outside the cockpit.

I ejected at about 5,500m altitude and the seat separated automatically, triggering the timer for the parachute, but the parachute opened automatically only at 1,500m. It was a long way down. I fell like a stone and could see the ground approaching so I opened the parachute manually because I thought I had gone below the altitude at which it would deploy automatically. We only had theoretical training in how to use parachutes. Then I was jerked into the upright position and it felt as if had stopped falling completely. On the way down I had lots of time to think. I was over Abu Aweigla and I could see el-Arish in the distance, burning. I decided to head towards a brown-topped hill which was in the direction of el-Arish.[13]

Another Egyptian formation reached all the way to around el-Arish in an attempt to intercept some dozens of Israeli fighter-bombers that were active there. However, the EAF's radar coverage

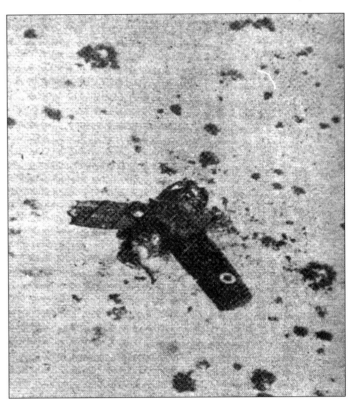

Wreckage of Fuad Kamal's MiG-15, as found by the Israelis after the ceasefire. (IDF):

An EAF MiG-15bis rolling for take-off before the war. Around noon on 31 October 1956, EAF MiG-15s fought a series of pitched air battles against Israeli Mystères and Ouragans over the Sinai peninsula. (Gabr Ali Gabr Collection)

Abd al-Rahman Muharram's MiG-15bis after the Israelis recovered it from Lake Bardawil after the Suez War. Its serial probably 1901 has been removed. (IDF)

over this area was grossly decreased by the loss of the local radar station to an Israeli air strike, and thus a formation of four MiG-15s was taken by surprise by four Mystères. Fuad Kamal described the results of the following air combat, as related by one of his close friends:

Having graduated in 1955, Abd al-Rahman Muharram was one of [the] youngest pilots in our squadron. His aircraft was hit in its starboard wing but he escaped from the Israelis after being hit by going down to extremely low altitude, flying at 'zero feet' and making abrupt manoeuvres. Before ditching in Lake Bardawil

A close-up view of the underside of an EAF MiG-15bis. Clearly visible is the size of the national insignia typical for the batch delivered within the frame of the 'Czech Arms Deal' and distribution of identification stripes. (Tahsin Zaki Collection)

there were no enemy aircraft close to him and the story that an Israeli flew alongside and could see the MiG pilot's face is nonsense.'

Much later, the Israelis found the ditched MiG, salvaged the aircraft and brought it to Israel for testing. Its photographs appear in most accounts of the 1956 War. Muharram's MiG eventually ended as trophy at the entrance to Hatzor AB.

During that afternoon, the EAF launched two additional operations over the Sinai peninsula, both involving large formations. Around 1530, four MiG-15bis launched from Kabrit to provide top cover for four Meteors from No. 5 Squadron sent in the direction of Jebel Libni. Underway there, they found a column of 202 Paratroop Brigade, which had been redirected from Mitla in the direction of Bir Gifgafa. Flying as Number 4 in the Meteor formation was Ala'a Barakat, who recalled the high point of his second and last combat sortie of the Suez War as follows:

We attacked a column of motorised infantry using rockets and then guns. I delivered a very precise strike, blew up an ammunition truck and strafed enemy troops. Several other vehicles were hit too. It was a highly successful attack.[14]

About an hour later, 14 MiG-15s from Kabrit and Abu Suweir attacked Israeli ground troops in the Abu Aweigla sector. After expending all their bombs and rockets, the MiGs scared away a pair of Mystère IVAs.

By this time, the EAF believed that it had achieved air superiority over the Sinai peninsula. Such conclusions were based upon the number of claimed aerial victories, unmolested operations by dozens of MiGs deep over Sinai, reports about heavy losses to the Israeli air force in air combats and to the air defences of the Egyptian Army, but also to the first reports – true or not – about a supposed involvement of Israel-based F-84Fs of the French air force. From the Egyptian point of view, there was no reason for French fighter-bombers to get involved on the Israeli side if the IDF/AF had been operating effectively. Although now preoccupied with the new threat of an Anglo-French invasion from the north, the EAF launched about 120 combat sorties (making 31 October the busiest day of the Suez War), fought about a dozen air combats and claimed at least six aerial victories against the IDF/AF, including three Ouragans and a

Mustang, while losing two MiG-15s in return.

With hindsight, this appears overoptimistic – and woul certainly be disputed by the Israelis. However, contrary to wha wa subsequently reported about the war, the EAF was far from bein seriously concerned about its position vis-à-vis the IDF/AF, and wa even further away from being defeated.

7
ANGLO-FRENCH ASSAULT

British bombing raids on Egypt began soon after nightfall on th evening of 31 October. Putting priority on knocking out four majo Egyptian air bases at Abu Suweir, Almaza, Inchas and Kabrit. Vicker Valiant and Canberra bombers of the RAF saturated these with larg numbers of 500lb and 1,000lb (225/400kg) bombs released from altitudes up to 40,000ft.[1] Cairo IAP was also hit, accidentally an despite the intention to spare it because it did not have any fighters and because US citizens were evacuated along the nearby highway Less than three hours later, Canberras hit Almaza again and fo the first time met light anti-aircraft fire, while the lights of th neighbouring Egyptian capital were finally switched off.

The air strike on Almaza ruined an Egyptian plan – based upon Nasser's order – to use about 20 Curtiss C-46 Command transports of No. 7 Squadron to drop the Egyptian Paratroop Brigad on the Mitla Pass during the night of 31 October to 1 November Fifteen of the 20 C-46s were destroyed by British bombs. Th Commander of No. 7 Squadron then led the pilots of the fiv remaining Commandos to an airfield in upper Egypt, where the survived the war.[2] Nevertheless, midway through the air strike, th EAF launched its final offensive sorties of the Suez War, in the form of two Il-28s tasked with bombing Tel Nov AB in Israel. The two bombers were piloted by Wing Commander Hamid Abdel-Ghafa and Mustafa Hilmi. EAF historian Labib explains:

I organised their take-offs and landings with help of the radar, so that these took place in between each wave of British bombardments.

Labib's synchronisation of these operations with Britist bombardments was anything but flawless. Hilmi crashed on take-off, leaving Abdel-Ghafar and his crew to continue the missior alone. Reportedly, they caught the Israelis by surprise, and found that the landing lights at Tel Nov were still on when dropping thei bombs. The Egyptian pilot returned to Cairo West, only to find the place under another attack by RAF bombers. He landed in complete darkness as British bombs were going off around him.

Nevertheless, the overall results of nocturnal British air raid were minimal. Very little damage was caused even to the runways and except for the C-46s, few other Egyptian aircraft were hit. Ever so, Egypt's limited night defences were put under immense stress and proved unable to cope. As far as is known, the EAF launche only two night-interceptor sorties that night, both by Meteo NF.Mk 13s. Squadron Leader Salah ed-Din Husayn, CO of the EAF's only night-fighter unit, intercepted the Valiant flown by Squadron Leader Ware of No. 148 Squadron, RAF, forcing him into violent evasive action. As Ware recalled:

The night-fighter came in to attack firing bursts of tracer. We took swift evasive action and the fighter fell away below us.[3]

Crews of Egyptian Il-28s preparing for a nocturnal sortie, sometimes in the late 1950s. While their attempts to attack IDF/AF air bases during the Suez War were often completely denied, at least some of them did reach Israel, but seem to have misidentified their targets. (Nour Bardai Collection)

Wing Commander Hamid Abdel-Ghafar, who flew the nocturnal attack on 'Aqir' (Tel Nov) air base during the night from 31 October to 1 November 1956. (Nour Bardai Collection)

A rare, pre-war photograph of the EAF Meteor NF.Mk 13 serial number 1428. Reportedly, only two of these fighters were operational during the 1956 Suez War. (David Nicolle Collection)

Husayn claimed to have scored a few hits, and the *Sawt al-Arab* radio station later exaggerated this into a confirmed kill, but the British bomber escaped unharmed. Similarly, a Canberra bombing Inchas was almost intercepted by a second Meteor NF.Mk 13, but the greatly superior performance of the British bomber at high altitude meant that the Egyptian pilot failed to approach close enough to open fire.

Wing Commander Mustafa Hilmi, CO of No. 9 Squadron EAF, was killed when his bomber crashed on take-off for a mission over Israel on the evening of 1 November 1956. (Nour Bardai Collection)

Left-hand view of a highly-convincing wooden replica of a MiG-15.
(David Nicolle Collection)

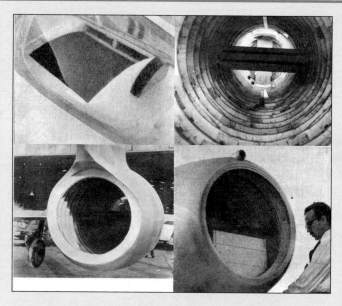

A collage of four photographs, detailing construction of one of the
wooden replica MiG-15s used as a decoy during the Suez War.
(Nour Bardai Collection)

DUMMY MiGs

Despite better preparedness in the air-to-air arena than is usually assessed, the EAF operational plan was entirely defensive and emphasised dispersal of aircraft and their redeployment to airfields in southern Egypt should the need arise. Also the major impact of the 'Czech Arms Deal' was that Egyptians began importing the essentially defensive Soviet air warfare doctrine. Even if it did not fit the conditions and environment of the Middle East, this doctrine emphasised air defence first, followed by air superiority and offensive air support. This is why the EAF mainly bought large numbers of interceptor aircraft designed to combat bombers, such as MiG-15s, trainers and transports, while acquiring only one offensive type, the Il-28. Even then, the General Command of the Egyptian military decided that air strikes on Israeli air bases were to be ordered only in the case of an Israeli attack on air bases west of the Suez Canal.[113]

Curiously, after realising that its own airfields were vulnerable to enemy air strikes, the EAF did very little to fortify them. Instead, it deployed several dozen excellently built wooden replica MiG-15s and Vampires on all major air bases. Their appearance and high quality would result in massively exaggerated claims by British and French pilots during the war.

As well as MiG decoys, the EAF deployed a number of highly convincing Vampire replicas. This one not only included an authentic serial 1562 but was also 'destroyed' by Israeli fighter-bombers during an attack on el-Arish AB. (Zionist Foundation)

Early on 1 November 1956, Squadron Leader el-Hinnawy led a formation of four MiG-17Fs from No. 1 Squadron, EAF, into their only known air strike on Israeli positions on the Sinai peninsula. (Shalaby el-Hinnawy Collection)

A trio of MiG-17Fs from No. 1 Squadron, EAF, as seen while underway over the deserts east of Cairo. (David Nicolle Collection)

A CRUEL DAY

1 November 1956 proved to be a very cruel day for the EAF, although arguably it started with an unexpected success. Early on the morning of 1 November, several Canberra PR.Mk 7s returned over Egypt to take reconnaissance photographs for post-strike analysis. One of them was intercepted and damaged by MiG-17Fs from No. 1 Squadron. The British aircraft returned safely to base, but this made it clear that the EAF's interceptor capability had not been destroyed. Indeed, the EAF even found the opportunity to launch several air strikes on Israeli forces in Sinai. Squadron Leader el-Hinnawy described the mission flown by a 'special group' of MiG-17s, which had only joined his squadron from the USSR the previous day:

> At first light on 1 November, I led a flight of four MiG-17s in a strafing attack against an Israeli position near Mitla Defile. The Israelis were dug in and well camouflaged – exactly like sand –

and were very difficult to see. We started firing and caused several explosions. We finished our ammunition and turned back.

Immediately afterwards, Egyptian air bases found themselves on the receiving end of a seemingly endless stream of air strikes flown by British and French fighter-bombers based in Cyprus and on aircraft carriers in the Mediterranean. Abu Suweir, Almaza and Kabrit experienced a series of particularly heavy and persistent attacks.

Being a temporary home for no less than 45 MiG-15s destined for Syria, as well as a number of EAF aircraft, Abu Suweir was one of the most frequently and heavily hit air bases. Farouq el-Ghazzawi recalled the first air strike:

> It was a lovely place, full of beautiful gardens. We were just finished breakfast and I was about to go to the squadron when we were caught. I remember seeing four Sea Hawks come in and strafe our aircraft. I was face down in one of the gardens and looked up and watched the jets hitting us.

Hard on the heels of fighter-bombers, Israel-based F-84Fs of the French air force rocketed and strafed Abu Suweir, before Commandante André Pichoff, assigned to the Escadron de Chasse 1/3 Navarre, encountered an EAF Meteor airborne over the air base. Pichoff opened fire, but failed to hit his target: the Egyptian quickly landed and rolled out of the sight of the French pilot.[5] Eventually, up to 20 assembled SyAAF MiGs were destroyed, while all the examples from the second Syrian MiG-15 order were damaged, although they escaped destruction.[6]

A similar series of air strikes hit Almaza, where Hinnawy was in the process of preparing another attack on the Israelis:

Civilians and members of the National Guard manhandling a wooden replica MiG-15 around one of the bombed out EAF air bases. Multiple reports by British and French pilots indicate that well-placed decoys attracted lots of attention. (David Nicolle Collection)

Most British and French accounts about air strikes on EAF air bases, flown on 1 November 1956, cite destruction of 'neat rows' of Egyptian MiGs. Whether their targets were genuine aircraft lined-up, as on this pre-war photograph of MiG-15s from Abu Suweir AB, or decoys, remains a matter of dispute. (Nour Bardai Collection)

I was giving a briefing to my pilots. At this moment we saw four aircraft – Sea Hawks – come in and strafe. Unfortunately, our MiG-17s were sitting in the open. The attack met with very weak anti-aircraft fire and many of our aircraft were wrecked. I remember seeing one Il-28 jet blow up. A shell splinter from the strafing hit me in the leg. I was ordered to go to the hospital for surgery but I refused.

Some eight of our MiGs covered by the camouflage nets near the hangars weren't hit in that first attack. We wanted to evacuate them but couldn't get approval from headquarters, and they were destroyed in subsequent raids.

However, contrary to Hinnawy's recollection, his unit must have received an order to evacuate, as Lieutenant-Commander Eveleigh, who flew Sea Hawks from the aircraft carrier HMS *Albion*, recalled:

We were surprised by a flight of MiGs which climbed away from Almaza towards us, and as we were only straight-winged compared to their swept-wing high-performance, I can still recall the feeling of my squadron closing up tight on me on sighting them. We were apprehensive, to say the least, but they swept straight past … We can only assume they were being flown away to some nearby safe heaven.[7]

Furthermore, French F-84Fs based in Israel claimed to have shot

down an Il-28 over Egypt, later during the day, indicating that not all of bombers still present at Almaza had been destroyed in earlier strikes. Meteors of No. 5 Squadron were not as lucky. For unknown reasons, this unit was ordered to evacuate all of its aircraft from Fayid to Almaza between two waves of enemy air strikes. Once on the ground, all eight F.Mk 8s were destroyed, leaving Alaa Barakat and his colleagues with nothing left to do. Barakat then flew the unit's sole surviving Meteor T.Mk 7 to Cairo IAP.[8]

Cairo West was hit repeatedly, as recalled by Flight Lieutenant Mohammed Nabil al-Masry, one of the MiG pilots based there:

I was in the cockpit at Readiness Rate 1 and could take off and get into action if an enemy was to come. We had four MiG-15s near the start of the runway. However, the attack came without any warning and I only had a very narrow chance to jump out of my jet and run from the attacking aircraft. The jets were turning to the left towards me. My Number 2 asked me, 'What shall I do?' I yelled, 'Jump!' and ran to the right to get away from their guns. I got only 20 or 30m before my aircraft was destroyed. I didn't see my Number 2 after I ran, I saw that all four aircraft were in flames. After a while, I saw this young pilot come out of the flames not touched or burned, and he was still struggling with his parachute, which was bouncing left and right … It looked very funny at the time. No one saw us get out and they thought we were killed.[9]

At Kabrit AB, a De Havilland Venom pilot from the RAF's No. 8 Squadron attacked a Harvard – apparently being used as a 'unit hack' – shortly after the latter took off. As far as can be reconstructed with the help of available Egyptian sources, EAF pilot Abd el-Moneim Hafiz Muhammad Iwais was badly injured, though managing either to bail out or make an emergency landing, but he died in hospital three days later.

Dikhelia was exposed to similar treatment by fighter-bombers of the Royal Navy and then by those of the French Aéronavale. These raids did not find the MiG-15s which they had anticipated, and, in fact, only destroyed some antiquated Supermarine Sea Otter biplane amphibians and a Beechcraft C-45 Expeditor light transport. In

According to unconfirmed Egyptian reports, some of their older British-made fighters were dispersed on secondary airfields in the Suez Canal Zone, perhaps even on the Sinai peninsula, to avoid destruction by British and French air strikes. This pre-war photograph of a Meteor F.Mk 4 shows details of national insignia, identification stripes and even the serial number applied on the underside of its wings. (Tom Cooper Collection)

frustration, some of the British pilots even strafed the large crates they saw on the airfield, in the hope that they still contained unassembled MiGs. Finally, later during the day, AdA F-84Fs based in Israel seem to have claimed their only aerial victory, when they intercepted an Il-28 over Egypt.[10]

However, beyond destroying the EAF on the ground, this British and French aerial bombardment had a huge impact on the Egyptian officer corps, those officers who used to have social ties to the RAF being shattered by these events. They not only felt betrayed by those they had regarded as friends, but were appalled by having to watch the enemy flying overhead while wondering why something was not done to stop them.

In total, the British and French pilots participating in assaults on Egyptian air bases on 1 November claimed the destruction of 82 MiG-15s and 73 other aircraft, the probable destruction of 20 MiGs and nine other aircraft, and damage to 41 MiGs and 85 other aircraft.[11]

NASSER'S DECISIONS

As their air raids continued with increasing intensity through the day, the British and French took control of Egypt's skies. The fact that the EAF did not attempt to intercept them was, at that time, attributed to low morale or even cowardice, and eventually lead to the conclusion that the Egyptian Air Force had been completely destroyed.[12] Only later did it become known that Egyptian pilots and ground personnel wanted to fight back, but were specifically ordered not to fly – at least not for the time being – by President Nasser, as he himself later explained:

We had 120 pilots fully trained for combat and [an]other 250 to 260 still in training. If I sent these to fight against the combined air forces of Britain and France I would have been mad … Planes can be replaced overnight, but it takes years to train a pilot.[13]

EAF historian Ali Muhammad Labib made essentially the same point:

Apart from their overwhelming numerical superiority, the enemy pilots were very experienced and were fully conversant with their aircraft. On the other side, the Egyptian jets were few in number and were flown by pilots who were new to their planes. As a result they had limited skill in manoeuvring their aircraft and of using the machines' full potential.

After touring the streets of Cairo to judge the mood of the people during the evening of 31 October, and knowing that Egypt's armed forces could not defeat three powerful invaders in open battle, President Nasser was worried enough to decide to start planning a guerrilla resistance. Realising that the Army would be exposed in the desert without air support, at 0730 on 1 November, he ordered a complete and immediate withdrawal of Egyptian ground units from Sinai. Until that moment, Israeli troop remained stalled in the Mitla Pass and northern Sinai, while Egyptian forces in the Gaza Strip were similarly still holding out. Field Marshal Amer and the General Command were hoping they could hold a line stretching from Lake Bardavil via the Giddi Pass down to the Mitla Defile, and even planned to redeploy some aircraft to a forward airstrip at Bir Gifgafa.[14] While most Egyptian commanders disagreed with their president, Nasser remained insistent, even when commanders of the Palestinian units in the Gaza Strip refused instructions to withdraw or surrender. While the EAF was either held back in the safety of its dispersal sites or, whenever possible, evacuated to southern Egypt, with the intention of operating as a sort of aerial guerrilla force, units of the Egyptian Army were forced to withdraw in a rush and without air cover, leaving much of their heavy equipment behind.

AERIAL GUERRILLA

By daylight on 2 November, Anglo-French air strikes had hit Luxor airfield again, resulting in a total claimed destruction of over 100 Egyptian aircraft, and caused serious disruption at most other air bases. Nevertheless, whenever possible, Egyptian and allied pilots continued to fly their aircraft out of the country or to evacuate them to remote dispersal sites to escape destruction, as explained by Barakat:

A reconnaissance photograph of Gamil airfield, with Port Said in the background. This was the scene of the last known operational sortie by an EAF fighter jet during the Suez War of 1956, flown by Nabil Kamil on the morning of 6 November. (Albert Grandolini Collection)

The MiG-17s redeployed from Almaza to a 2km-long stretch of straight road on the main road from Cairo to Alexandria. This was near Sindiyun, just before Benha, where the road ran alongside the dead-straight railway line. This was not a prepared road-strip but just a straight bit of road.

Fuad Kamal was also sent to a road-strip in the Delta:

We were sent to the Delta road connecting Cairo and Alexandria. We used some of the longer and wider stretches of road as runways. Here we only used MiGs. There were bunkers already there, camouflaged with greenery.

Farouq el-Ghazzawi recalled flying MiG-15s from the Cairo-Suez road, but his reference to this location may have been a slip in the memory or indicate that a straight stretch of road east of Almaza was also being used as another dispersal site.

Feeling that something else had to be attempted to remove the threat posed by Egypt's surviving Il-28s, at mid-morning of 2 November, a wave of F-84Fs attacked Luxor airfield with rockets and strafing, destroying or damaging six of the EAF bombers that were still there.

Once it was clear that the EAF had effectively been put out of action, Anglo-French commanders began considering the threat of air attacks on bases in Cyprus from the direction of Syria instead. Canberras and RF-84Fs were thus sent on reconnaissance missions over Syrian airfields. Amongst others, a British crew reported sighting four Il-28s at Damascus during the day.[15]

With the EAF out of the way, Allied Headquarters Cyprus decided to initiate phase two of the assault on Egypt. This was to be an air offensive coupled with psychological warfare intended to bring about a collapse of the Egyptian people's will to resist, and consequently the downfall of President Nasser. With a realisation that the latter would now not occur, the British and French concentrated upon attacking military targets. They also flew an air strike against the transmitters used to broadcast the *Sawt al-Ara'* ('The Voice of the Arabs') which was located at Abu Za'bal, a suburb of Cairo. Flown by 18 Canberras which approached at high speed and relatively low altitude, this strike caused substantial damage to the antenna farm, but proved less accurate than expected. Instead, several bombs hit the main Cairo Prison, killing nearly 100 prisoners and warders. Not only was the 'Voice of the Arabs' only off the air for a few brief hours, but the massacre of civilians at the prison caused such a public outcry that a French proposal of a further attack by F-84Fs was rejected.

Instead, British and French aircrew spent most of the day flying additional air strikes against EAF bases, as well as various other military installations. Eventually, their pilots claimed destruction of a further 28 MiGs and 28 other aircraft, the probable destruction of two MiGs and six other aircraft, and damage to 32 MiGs and 75 other aircraft.[16]

However, that evening, the British and French realised that the EAF, far from ceasing to exist, was up to something. Such assessments were based on photo-reconnaissance of Almaza AB, which showed a significant concentration of MiGs. The aircraft in question were apparently evacuated there from the Canal Zone. With other intelligence sources indicating that the EAF would be launching an unspecified number of aircraft from Almaza at first light, the Fleet Air Arm sent Sea Hawks to attack this base as early as possible on 3 November. However, their pilots found next to nothing to target.

Elsewhere during the day, the British and French continued striking Egyptian air bases and other military installations, and also added railway marshalling yards to their targets. By the end of 3 November, they claimed the destruction of another four MiGs and 17 other aircraft, plus damage to three MiGs and 22 other aircraft.[17]

In Sinai, the Israelis were busy with their operations against Sharm el-Sheik. After the local Egyptian garrison partially withdrew and partially capitulated, and with most other Egyptian Army units withdrawn from the peninsula, the war in Sinai was now practically over. With the situation on the Sinai peninsula under control, the commander of the AdA contingent in Israel, Commandante Perseval, requested permission to strike Luxor airfield. This was granted, and early that morning, 13 F-84Fs took off for their long trip. Apparently catching the Egyptians by surprise, the French found no less than 20 Il-28s on the ground and caused heavy damage. Around noon, six additional F-84Fs repeated this attack, followed by a single RF-84F from Cyprus, which photographed the results of the air strikes. In total, the French claimed the destruction of 17 EAF aircraft at Luxor that day, including at least 10 Il-28s. Egyptian sources confirmed that six Il-28s were destroyed and that Usama Sidki then flew one of the last remaining bombers to Jeddah in Saudi Arabia.

In recognition of the fact that the EAF was not yet neutralised, Anglo-French operations on 4 and 5 November targeted not only air bases, but also radar stations and military positions in areas about to be targeted by the airborne assault. But the pilots involved could find hardly any Egyptian aircraft on EAF air bases, let alone be able to destroy any. Even so, the destruction of three MiGs on the ground was claimed on 4 November, and another five on the following day.

Clearly, days of continuous bombardment had begun to take a serious toll on the morale of the Egyptian military and its leaders. On the other hand, the situation witnessed a sudden improvement on 5 November, when it became known that London and Paris were now under increasing pressure from the USA and Soviet Union to stop their assault and withdraw. Outraged that the Anglo-French invasion had been launched shortly before presidential elections in the USA, and considering that the US public in general was against such military interventions, Eisenhower sponsored a UN resolution denouncing the attack on Egypt. Issued on 2 November, this called for an immediate ceasefire and was followed by US threats to cancel vital loans to its European allies. In an attempt to create a *fait accompli*, Anglo-French forces launched a rushed invasion of Port Said and then pushed on down both sides of the Suez Canal on 5/6 November. With most of the Egyptian Army withdrawn from Sinai and still intact, despite heavy losses to air strikes, Nasser concluded that Port Said was indefensible and withdrew most of the regular troops from the city, leaving only local militia and armed civilians to harass the invaders.

SURPRISE OF 6 NOVEMBER

The final day of the Suez War was 6 November, and because the EAF had made no appearance on the previous two days, it was generally assumed to have ceased to exist. It thus came as quite a surprise when EAF MiG-15s appeared over the battlefield west of Port Said to demonstrate that the EAF was still around. At dawn, the British, who had taken control of Gamil airfield, were suddenly strafed by a MiG-15. Several RAF Venoms tried to give chase, and one of them approached to within less than 200m before the EAF fighter accelerated away.

The aircraft in question was piloted by Flight Officer Nabil Kamil from No. 1 Squadron, who flew one of two MiG-15s that took off from a stretch of road near Benha, as recalled by Barakat:

There were two MiGs, and Nabil Kamil was the leader of that mission. One of them returned with 32 bullet holes from small-arms fire.

Recalling the 'special purpose' of the mission in question, Fuad Kamal concluded:

It was undertaken just to show that the Egyptian Air Force still existed, nothing else.

By that time, it was clear that a ceasefire was about to be imposed and therefore Egypt wanted to send a signal that it had not been defeated. A more immediate result of Kamil's mission was that the British reacted by establishing a standing combat air patrol of Sea Hawks, and even RAF Hunters based on Cyprus were sent in fighter sweeps over the Nile Delta. At least one of the pilots involved did sight a swept-wing fighter later in the morning, thought to have been an EAF MiG, but was unable to intercept because the aircraft was flying at high speed in the opposite direction. The re-appearance of the EAF caused some additional air strikes to be made against air bases, as a result of which British and French pilots claimed the destruction of two MiGs and five other aircraft, the probable destruction of one other aircraft, and damage to five MiGs and 16 other aircraft before the UN-imposed ceasefire came into force, ending further action.

CANBERRA DOWN

Most claims for air combat victories by Egyptian pilots against Israeli and British aircraft during the Suez War are disputed to one degree or the other. Only one loss was never disputed; that of an RAF Canberra PR.Mk 7 from No. 13 Squadron on 6 November. While not taking place over Egypt, nor involving the EAF, the affair did see Egyptian involvement, although contemporary British reports usually credited this downing to MiG-15s supposedly flown by Czechoslovak or Soviet advisors.

As described earlier, the British had started flying reconnaissance sorties over Syria in late October 1956. Rumours such as the one about the arrival of '123 MiGs' in Damascus caused genuine concerns in Cyprus, and thus the British were anxious to find out what was really going in Syria.

Officially established on 16 October 1946, and subsequently experiencing similar problems to those faced by the EAF when it came to the acquisition of modern combat aircraft, the Syrian Arab Air Force of 1956 was ill-equipped to counter such incursions. Most

of its aircraft were of British origin and had been acquired within the framework of a big order placed in January 1950. This had stipulated the delivery of about a dozen Chipmunk trainers, 10 Spitfire F.Mk 22s, 12 Meteor F.Mk 8s and two Meteor T.Mk 7s. Although London granted permission for the delivery of Chipmunks and Spitfires, along with the training of two groups of Syrian pilots and ground personnel, deliveries of Meteors were blocked for several years. Thus, it was only between September 1952 and March 1953 that Syria received its first 12 jet fighters. In the summer of 1954, the SyAAF placed a further order for six ex-RAF Meteor NF.Mk 13s but these arrived without their radar equipment and were used as dual-control conversion trainers instead. Organised into No. 9 Squadron, the 12 Meteor F.Mk 8s thus remained the primary Syrian interceptors as of 1956, when highly experienced Egyptian fighter pilot Tahir Zaki was ordered to Syria to serve as an instructor pilot:

I had been sent to help the Syrians. They had good pilots but had no knowledge or training in air combat … they were very grateful … There were two English instructors in Damascus when I first arrived in Syria. They were training the Syrians to fly Meteors, but they did not teach them air combat … We also taught them to support their Army by ground strafing. The Syrians became particularly good at this afterwards.'[18]

As of October 1956, the majority of experienced SyAAF pilots and ground personnel were undergoing conversion courses for MiGs at Bilbeis AB in Egypt. Nevertheless, Tahir Zaki was still in Syria, training others, including Lieutenant Hafez al-Assad.

I was sent to Syria again in early 1956. It was probably in February … I was flying in a two-seater Meteor with Hafez al-Assad when one of [the] tyres burst [on take-off]. I think it was the left. I told Assad that both of us must push the rudder to keep the aircraft straight when we landed. We got down OK. Assad was a good pilot.

When the Suez War erupted, Tahir Zaki was still in Damascus and was kept fully informed about enemy operations, including their reconnaissance overflights over Syria. The SyAAF had not a single early warning radar in service at that time. However, by colating telephone calls from local police stations which reported Canberras above Latakia, Aleppo, Homs and even Damascus, one of the Syrian ground controllers, Major Moukabri, concluded that the British did not always follow the same route. By taking a sequence of telephone calls, he could gauge the bearings of the enemy aircraft, deduce their tracks and approximate speed. In cooperation with Zaki, he developed a plan to intercept one of the involved aircraft along its extrapolated line of flight.

Shortly after 0800 on 6 November, the Syrian frontier post with Iraq at Abu Kamal, on the Euphrates River, telephoned to announce a Canberra approaching from within Iraqi airspace. Lieutenant Assad was scrambled immediately and managed to approach closely enough to open fire from a distance, before the British reconnaissance aircraft escaped towards Cyprus. The crew of the Canberra intercepted by Assad found its target covered with cloud, and thus the headquarters in Cyprus ordered another reconnaissance mission. This was flown by the crew of Flight Lieutenant B.L. Hunter, which had already experienced interception by an Egyptian MiG early on 30 October.

Launching at 1230, Hunter first piloted his Canberra at an altitude between 10,000-12,000ft over Riyaq AB in Lebanon, before overflying Nayrab AB near Aleppo in Syria and then Rashid AB, near Baghdad in Iraq. By this time, SyAAF Meteor pilots were practically living in their cockpits, and thus when Hunter's jet reappeared within Syrian airspace at around 1600, it did not take long to scramble six interceptors from Nayrab and Mezze on the outskirts of Damascus. They included aircraft flown by al-Assad, al-Garudy and al-Assassa, the CO of the Meteor squadron.

There is some contradiction between Syrian and Egyptian accounts at this point, since it remains unclear whether Garudy and Assassa formed a pair, or were each leading a different pair of Meteors. The latter was probably the case, because the Syrians subsequently concluded they shot down two Canberras, while Hunter's Canberra crew believed they had been attacked by two different pairs of Meteors. Tahir Zaki concluded:

When the Canberra passed over Lattakia they telephoned us in Damascus and we told the pilots to start their engines and take off. The Canberra was over Aleppo by then. There was usually low cloud over Damascus at that time of the day during that time of year, so we told the pilots to stay hidden in these clouds. When they got the message that the Canberra had passed over Homs they were to climb out of the clouds and prepare to attack. The result was a successful interception.

Major Moukabri later recalled that his pilots could initially not the see the Canberra until they were advised to look downwards. Then the first pair approached from port to starboard, and made a stern attack. Hunter turned his aircraft towards the two Syrians and evaded them. However, another pair then came in, and while turning into them, the Canberra's right engine received a hit and caught fire. Rapidly losing control of the situation, the British pilot ordered his crew to eject. His Canberra crashed just inside Syrian territory; one crewmember came down by parachute inside Syria, while Hunter himself landed inside Lebanon, in turn prompting Tahir Zaki to conclude that the survivors were two pilots from two different Canberras. The third member of the RAF crew was killed in the crash.

Meteors of the SyAAF remained on alert for the rest of the day, and about 40 minutes before sunset on 6 November, Hafez al-Assad was again scrambled in pursuit of another intruder. The identity of the aircraft in question remains unknown, but it was most likely a Lockheed U-2 – because it is known that the CIA was also looking for the '100 or so' MiGs supposedly deployed to Syria.

The young Syrian pilot tested his brakes before taking off and found them faulty, but took off anyway. After being unable to find the intruder, apparently due to the failure of his radio, Assad was forced to land in darkness at an air base that had no night-flying aids. He could hardly see the runway, and the wind direction had changed during his flight. As a result, Assad landed downwind, and, with his faulty brakes unable to cope, overshot. The Meteor smashed through a small orchard and headed for a stone wall. Assad opened the cockpit hood while steering with the rudder, was bounced over the wall by a water conduit and just missed the tents of a Palestinian refugee camp. Eventually, his aircraft smashed down again, tearing off its undercarriage, and came to rest on its belly. He was subsequently reprimanded and given a suspended jail sentence for taking off with defective brakes, thus endangering a precious aircraft.

British reconnaissance flights over Syria continued after the Suez War, but the Canberras were henceforth escorted by Hawker Hunters of Nos 1 and 34 Squadrons. Similarly, French RF-84Fs were only sent over Syria in pairs.

THE FINAL TALLY

From the Egyptian perspective, the Suez conflict did not end on 7 November 1956, but lasted another 120 days, until the Anglo-French forces had completed their withdrawal from Egyptian territory. Despite their claims to the contrary, the Israelis were not in the least eager to vacate the Sinai peninsula. It was only under severe pressure from the administration of US President Eisenhower that they eventually did so. As soon as the Israeli invasion of Egypt had became obvious on 31 October, Eisenhower had terminated all development and technical assistance to Israel, along with all shipments of agricultural products, all forms of loan and all military assistance. Facing national bankruptcy, Ben-Gurion had to withdraw Israeli troops not only from official Egyptian territory, but also from the Palestinian Gaza Strip. Even then, the IDF did not leave before summarily executing dozens of the 4,000-strong 8th (Palestinian) Division and their Egyptian officers, as well as killing between 930 and 1,200 other people in Gaza, by March 1957.[19]

From the EAF's point of view, the conflict had caused significant damage to its air bases, but had not inflicted the crippling losses claimed by the British, French and Israelis. For example, the British and French claimed the destruction of no less than 124 MiG-15s and MiG-17s in six days of air strikes against Egyptian air bases. The final British tally for the number of EAF aircraft supposedly destroyed stood at 91 out of a total of 110 MiGs, 11 out of 14 Meteors, 30 out of 44 Vampires and 26 or 27 Il-28s. Israel claimed to have shot down four MiGs and four Vampires in air combat on 30 and 31 October. Therefore, the Egyptian air force should have been completely wiped out.

However, despite the fact that Egypt never published an official list of its losses during the 1956 Suez War, there is some information in relation to British-made aircraft. As mentioned above, the last eight operational Meteor F.Mk 8s are known to have been destroyed at Almaza on 1 November, while the sole remaining T.Mk 7 is known to have been donated to Syria after the war. The ultimate fate of most of the other Meteors and Vampires remains unknown. Reports from available Egyptian and Saudi sources indicate that at least seven Vampires were subsequently sold to Saudi Arabia.[20] A small number of Meteor F.Mk 4s might have survived, too. At least one example – serial number 1410 – was photographed at Almaza in 1959, already wearing the red, white and black insignia of the United Arab Republic Air Force, established a year earlier through the union of Egypt, Syria and Yemen. It is unlikely that a solitary example would be kept in operational condition by that date, though it may have been used for ground instruction. Similarly, at least two Miles Magisters remained in service at Bilbeis and were last photographed in 1959.

The situation is only slightly better regarding the EAF's MiG fleet. For example, it is known that the EAF returned 32 MiG-15bis and 6 MiG-17Fs to its battered air bases during November and December 1956. This would mean that almost exactly 50 percent of the fleet survived the war. Furthermore, while Czechoslovak documentation confirmed the destruction of all 21 MiG-15bis from the first batch delivered to Egypt (four MiG-15UTIs were successfully evacuated during the war), it also shows that all of the 20 Syrian-ordered MiG-15bis that arrived in Egypt in October 1956 survived the Suez War.[21]

The number of Il-28s which survived the Suez War is much more difficult to assess. Egyptian sources confirm the crash of one bomber during take-off from Cairo West on the evening of 31 October, along with the destruction of one bomber by British

A pre-delivery photograph of three Meteor F.Mk 8s (serials 402, 411 and 412) that did eventually reach Syria in late 1952 and early 1953. (Tom Cooper Collection)

A row of Syrian Meteor NF.Mk 13s in 1959. Delivered without their radar equipment, they served as conversion trainers instead. (Nour Bardai Collection)

This aircraft serial number 109 was one of 12 Meteor F.Mk 8s ordered by Syria in 1950 and embargoed by London. As far as is known, it never reached its destination. (Albert Grandolini Collection)

air strikes on Almaza AB on 1 November and the loss of six Il-28s at Luxor on 6 November. However, apart from the evacuation of about 20 Il-28s by Czechoslovak and Soviet instructors, and by Usama Sidqi, to Jeddah (including examples coded G, K, N, and M) in Saudi Arabia, the whereabouts of the remaining 17 aircraft of this type remain unclear.

The situation regarding EAF's MiGs and Ilyushins was further complicated by the fact that on 28 February 1957, Egypt and Czechoslovakia concluded another, final, large arms contract. According to Czechoslovak documentation, this included orders for 20 newly built and 10 second-hand Il-28s, two Il-28 conversion trainers, 77 MiG-17s, 30 MiG-15s, six MiG-15UTIs, 40 Yak-11 advanced trainers, 50 Zlin Z-226T basic trainers, 10 L-60 liaison aircraft, five Il-15 transports, five Mil Mi-1 light utility helicopters and five Mi-4 medium utility helicopters.[22] However, exactly how much of this order was ultimately realised remains unknown. For example, not only did the number of MiG-15bis and Il-28s in service with the EAF never increase again after December 1956, but the same contract stipulated delivery of 900 ZAB-250-130B napalm bombs – and Egypt is known to have had not a single napalm bomb before the mid-1970s.[23] What is certain is that 11 years later, on 5 June 1967, Egypt still operated 26 MiG-15bis and 34 Il-28s. If Egypt

Another pre-delivery photograph of SyAAF Meteor F.Mk 8s. As far as is known, all were camouflaged in olive green and light earth on upper surfaces and sides, and sky blue on undersides. Serials were applied in white on the upper part of the fins, and repeated in black on drop tanks. (Albert Grandolini Collection)

A formation of Mraz Sokols assigned to the Air Force College, seen in 1959. (Nour Bardai Collection)

Evidence of survival: this EAF Meteor F.Mk 4 serial number 1410 was photographed at Almaza AB in 1959, while already wearing the black, white and red national insignia of the United Arab Republic Air Force. (David Nicolle Collection)

A line-up of five MiG-17Fs and three MiG-15bis at the demolished Abu Suweir AB in November 1956. All of these survived the Suez War. (David Nicolle Collection)

had received additional aircraft of either type after December 1956, these figures would certainly have been much higher.[24]

The number of EAF training aircraft destroyed during the Suez War is even harder to assess. While it appears that most of the Chipmunks were knocked out during air strikes at Bilbeis AB, it is known that enough Harvards survived to remain in service as advanced trainers at the Air Force College into the early 1960s. The last few aircraft might have been Syrian aircraft obtained when Egypt and Syria joined together as the United Arab Republic in 1958, and most of the Syrian Arab Air Force's equipment was moved to Egypt. Following their withdrawal from service with the Air Force Academy in 1961 or 1962, the last few Harvards were attached to various squadrons as communications or liaison aircraft. Even then, at least a handful remained in service and one is known to have been destroyed during Israeli air strikes on Fayd AB on 5 June 1967.

What is also certain is that Egyptian personnel losses were minimal, only six EAF pilots being known to have been killed during the Suez War, as detailed in Table 5.

Unsurprisingly, despite the massive loss of aircraft and heavy losses of recently acquired tanks of Soviet origin, the Egyptians concluded that the Suez War had culminated in a clear-cut victory for Egypt. Cairo had achieved its political objectives in becoming the de facto owner of the Suez Canal, with the exclusive right to operate it without any interference or objection from abroad. For Britain and France, their last gasps of colonialism in the Middle East were

an unqualified disaster, with far-reaching geopolitical consequences, as concluded by Tawil:

We felt angry about 1956 and everyone wanted Egypt to beome strong enough to resist if it happened again. Our motivation was very strong, particularly in my generation which had been brought up on stories of the Battle of Britain. We identified very strongly with the RAF of 1940. We felt that Egypt was too weak and we felt that we had been betrayed by the British.

Instead of removing Nasser, the tripatrite aggression made him more popular and powerful than ever before or since, while it was the British and French leaders, Anthony Eden and Guy Mollet, who would be ousted by the summer of 1957. Indeed, Egypt's international prestige grew enormously and Nasser became the undisputed figurehead of Arab nationalism until his death from a heart attack in 1970.

Although commonly portrayed as the nominal sole winner of the Suez conflict – apparently because of the substantial amount of materiel it captured in Sinai – Israel's involvement in the tripartite plot destroyed any chance of a negotiated settlement with the Arabs for dozens of years to come.

Table 5: Confirmed Losses of EAF Pilots during the Suez War, 1956

Date	Rank & Name	Notes
29 October	Sqn Ldr Mustafa Mahmud Ismail	Pilot of Il-14 shot down by IDF/AF Meteor NF.Mk 13
29 October	Sqn Ldr Kamal ad-Din Ahmad Abu l'-Rahim	Co-pilot of Il-14 shot down by IDF/AF Meteor NF.Mk 13
31 October	Sqn Ldr Bahgat Hassan Hilmi	Pilot of Vampire FB.Mk 52 shot down by IDF/AF Mystère
31 October	Plt Off Mahmmoud Wael Afifi	Pilot of Vampire FB.Mk 52 shot down by IDF/AF Mystère
31 October	Flt Off Ahmad Faghal	Pilot of Vampire FB.Mk 52 shot down by IDF/AF Mystère
31 October	Wg Cdr Mustafa Hilmi	Il-28-pilot, crashed on take-off from Cairo West; fate of other two crewmembers unknown

FORGOTTEN LESSONS

The Egyptian military should have learned a number of very important lessons from the Suez War, but failed to do so. Instead, some basic weaknesses in the Egyptian military appeared in 1956 and would remain typical of its methods of fighting for the next 20 years.

Although the EAF proved more than capable of operating brand-new equipment on its own, certainly more than had been expected by almost everybody, the flow of war forced it into a reactive mode right from the start. The Egyptian Air Force thus acted to defend its airspace, defending Egyptian Army troops on Sinai and striking at enemy troops. At the same time, its offensive capabilities remained underdeveloped, if not actually non-existent. Much more than this, however, for the majority of Egyptians – and indeed for the entire Arab world – the memory of a crushing military defeat by Anglo-French air power during the Suez War was soon erased by euphoria over Egypt's political victory. Under heavy pressure from the United States, France and Great Britain were forced to leave the Suez Canal and concede its sovereignty to Egypt, while Israel was forced to return to the ceasefire lines established early in 1949.

On the other hand, because Egypt regained Sinai without a fight and its military power was relatively rapidly rebuilt, the Egyptians began to ignore many realities and also failed to draw useful lessons. In the case of the EAF, there were almost countless instances of such failures. For example, while most Egyptian aircraft were destroyed on the ground as a result of strafing by cannons or rocket fire, the EAF undertook next to nothing to improve protection of its aircraft on the ground, nor to fortify its bases. Instead of studying weaknesses of the MiG-15bis and MiG-17F more closely, the EAF rushed to replace its losses in older jets of British origin with additional MiG-17Fs, without paying attention to modifying or further developing these aircraft by drawing upon experiences from the Suez War. While some of this could be explained by realising that the majority of Egyptian pilots were inexperienced novices who would not be in a position to learn such lessons, it should nevertheless not have happened.

At a tactical level, at least according to Israeli reports, EAF MiG-pilots seemingly began to follow Soviet advice and started using some of the tactics already seen amongst Soviet, Chinese and North Korean pilots over Korea. Contrary to the British-trained Meteor and Vampire pilots who flew in 'finger four' formations and sought to use the manoeuvrability of their aircraft, the MiG pilots used staggered formations at various altitudes. They disengaged with climbing turns when under attack, although most Egyptian pilots actually reported disliking such manoeuvres. Furthermore, their aircraft lacked power-assisted controls and tight turns therefore not only exposed them to high g-forces, but also tired them rapidly.

Yet it has to be admitted that the biggest problems were related to issues over which the Egyptians had very little control, or at least it would have taken immense effort on the part of the EAF for the Soviets to react appropriately. The problems in question were all related to the design, and especially to the armament, of their MiGs. Unsurprisingly, considering the background of their designer and their original purpose was to intercept bombers such as the US-made Boeing B-29 Superfortress – the MiG-15 and MiG-17 were optimised for high-altitude operations. Whenever deployed at low

Table 6: Claimed, Probable and Confirmed Aerial Victories by EAF, Suez War, 1956

Date	EAF Aircraft & Crew	Target	Result of Attack
30 October	MiG-15bis, Flt Lt Sayd al-Qadi, No. 1 Squadron	Canberra PR.Mk 7	port elevator damaged or narrowly missed
30 October	MiG-15bis, Flt Lt Hussayn Sidki, MiG OTU	Mystère IVA	severely damaged
30 October	MiG-15bis, Sqn Ldr Nazih Khalifa, No. 30 Squadron	Piper Cub	shot down, pilot KIA*
31 October	MiG-15ibs, Sqn Ldr Nazih Khalifa, No. 30 Squadron	Ouragan	severely damaged
31 October	Vampire FB.Mk 52, Flt Lt Zuhayr, No. 31 Squadron	P-51D Mustang	shot down, pilot KIA*
31 October	MiG-15bis, Flt Lt Farouq el-Ghazzawi, No. 30 Squadron	Ouragan	severely damaged
31 October	Meteor NF.Mk 13, Sqn Ldr Salah ed-Din Husayn, No. 10 Squadron	Valiant B.Mk 1	missed
			(*killed in action)

altitudes, they proved true 'gas-guzzlers'. This was obvious from their combat radius. A MiG-15 loaded with two external fuel tanks and two 250kg bombs could only reach targets 230 miles away from its base if underway at high altitude. This reduced to 120 miles at medium, and only 85 miles if underway at low altitude all the time. Although larger and more powerful, the MiG-17F offered no advantages in this regards. If loaded with two external fuel tanks and two 250kg bombs, it could reach 210 miles at high altitude, 145 at medium and 90 miles at low altitude.

This very limited endurance during low-altitude operations proved one of the biggest shortcomings of EAF MiG-17s during the Suez War. Furthermore, because the aircraft needed two drop tanks to reach most of their targets in the Sinai peninsula, and because these drop tanks were jettisoned whenever the aircraft engaged in combat, their expenditure was excessively high. Indeed, all three EAF units which operated MiG-15s ran out of drop tanks after only two or three major combat operations. The shortage of drop tanks became widespread as early as the afternoon of 31 October.

Furthermore, the jettisoning of the tanks often proved dangerous. If only one separated, a MiG-15 easily slipped into a spin, especially during violent combat manoeuvres or if the pilot applied an emergency method of detaching reluctant tanks. Even if the pilot recovered, spinning with a single drop tank often caused severe wing deformation.

The major deficiency of these early MiGs was their armament. Each MiG-15bis and MiG-17F was armed with two NR-23 guns. These had a rate of fire of 850-950rpm and were relatively jam-proof, but the muzzle velocity of their shells was rather low, at 690m/sec (2,264ft/sec), as was their rate of fire, which was only 550-700 rounds per minute (rpm). While this was partially equalised by the mass output of 1.8kg/sec (4lb/sec) forr each NR-23, the fact was that in a turning air combat, their shells were less likely to score a hit. The third cannon on both MiG-15bis and MiG-17F was the powerful N-37D. Although lighter, gas-operated and smaller than its predecessors, it fired projectiles at a similar muzzle velocity as the NR-23, which was 690m/sec (2,254ft/sec), at a rate of fire of 400rpm. The essence of all of this was that Soviet cannons tended to fire relatively heavy shells at a low rate of fire.[25]

Another issue related to this armament configuration was that shells fired by NR-23s and N-37s had entirely different trajectories, which in turn caused significant sighting problems. Hence, although the muzzle velocities of their shells were similar and the projectiles had a similar shape, their weight was significantly different: 23mm shells fired by NR-23s weighed 200g while those of the NR-37 weighed 700g. This resulted in a considerable difference in section density ratios and therefore in a different trajectory at long range.

From the standpoint of the MiG-designers, such armament perfectly suited interceptors designed to combat large and steady-flying targets like Boeing B-29s underway at high altitudes, which is what the MiG-15 was originally designed for. Indeed, the Soviets estimated that two 37mm or eight 23mm hits would be sufficient to destroy an aircraft such as a Boeing B-29, and that just one 37mm or two 23mm hits would bring down any fighter.[26] Because such targets were also large, differences in the flight trajectories of the NR-23's and N-37's shells were not expected to matter very much. Indeed, their spread over several metres was likely to cause even more damage.

However, the Suez War of 1956 proved such theories to be wrong – and, to make matters even more difficult, both the Egyptians and Soviets failed to realise this fact. Many Israeli fighters received 23mm and 37mm hits from Egyptian MiGs, but nevertheless returned

safely to their bases and, as far as is known, all were subsequently repaired.

Related to the issue of cannons was the amount of ammunition carried. All three cannons installed in the MiG-15 and MiG-17 were neatly packed into a container that was easy to dismount from the aircraft, reload with ammunition and reinstall. However, this container packed only 40 rounds for the N-37 and 80 for each of two NR-23s. This compared unfavourably with the amount of ammunition carried by all contemporary Western fighters, and meant that MiGs generally suffered from a significant shortage of ammunition, with their magazines usually being empty after only two or three short bursts.

Furthermore, while generally regarded as robust, highly reliable, simple to fly and to operate, the MiGs offered no advantage in these regards in comparison to the faster and slightly more manoeuvrable Mystère, nor even in regards to the slower but again more manoeuvrable Ouragan. Both of these French aircraft proved to be at least as robust and probably more reliable than the MiGs, while also having a very long service life.

Finally, French fighters carried much more effective and more homogenous armament with higher muzzle velocity and a higher rate of fire, which was more suitable for fighter versus fighter action, than did the MiGs. Mystère IVAs were equipped with 30mm DEFA 551 cannons (a further development of the German MK 213/30 from the Second World War), which had a muzzle velocity of up to 800m/sec (2,625ft/sec) and almost three times as high a rate of fire as either the NR-23 or N-37D. Ouragans were armed with four 20mm Hispano HS 404 cannon, experiences with which were so favourable that the IDF/AF massively expanded its Ouragan force after the Suez War.

Combined with better sights, power-assisted flight controls and an ammunition capacity of 150 shells per gun, this resulted in a situation where Israeli pilots could fire more often than Egyptian MiG pilots, and were more likely to score a hit on a fleeting target such as a hard-manoeuvring fighter jet. While the shells fired by DEFA 551s weighted less than 40 percent of those fired by the NR-37, they also proved more reliable. Although several Egyptian MiGs survived multiple hits, the three that were eventually shot down during the Suez War all succumbed to only between one and three hits.

The results of all of this should have been clear to the EAF. While Egyptian MiG pilots showed far more competence in their new aircraft than had been expected by almost everybody, they were far less likely to score kills in air combats against fast and manoeuvrable fighters, and were thus far less likely to establish air superiority, than were their Israeli opponents. Unfortunately, this fact remained unrecognised for another dozen years, with well-known and rather tragic repercussions – for Egypt, and the Arab world in general – in June 1967.

BIBLIOGRAPHY

Bull, General O., *War and Peace in the Middle East: the Experiences and Views of a UN Observer* (London: Leo Cooper Ltd, 1976) ISBN 0-85052-226-9

Burns, W., *Economic Aid and American Policy towards Egypt* (New York: State University of New York Press, 1985) ISBN 978-0-873958-69-1

Cohen, Colonel E. 'Cheetah', *Israel's Best Defence* (Shrewsbury: Airlife Publishing Ltd, 1993) ISBN 1-85310-484-1

Cooper, T., & Nicolle, D., *Arab MiGs, Volume 3* (Houston: Harpia Publishing LLC, 2012) ISBN 978-0-9825539-9-2

Cooper, T., Nicolle, D., & Nordeen, L., *Arab MiGs, Volume 4* (Houston: Harpia Publishing LLC, 2013) ISBN 978-0-985455-41-5

Cull, B., Nicolle, D., & Aloni, S., *Wings over Suez* (London: Grub Street, 1996) ISBN 1-898697-48-5

Denis, A., *Historique de l'escadron de chasse 13 Navarre: 19152000* (A. Denis, 2001) ASIN: B000WUR6DM

Eden, A., *Full Circle: The Memoirs of Anthony Eden* (Boston: Houghton Mifflin, 1960) ASIN: B0006AVZVM

Even, Y., 'Two Squadrons and their Pilots: The First Syrian Request for the Deployment of Soviet Military Forces on its Territory, 1956', *Cold War International History Project*, Working Paper No. 77 (Woodrow Wilson International Center for Scholars, February 2016)

Green, S., *Taking Sides: America's Secret Relations with a Militant Israel, 1948/1967* (London: Faber and Faber Ltd, 1984) ISBN 0-571-13271-5

Green, W., & Fricker, J., *The Air Forces of the World* (London: MacDonald, 1958) ASIN: B000XHOFYC

Laron, G., 'Cutting the Gordian Knot: The Post-WWII Egyptian Quest for Arms and the 1955 Czechoslovak Arms Deal', *Cold War International History Project*, Working Paper No. 55 (Woodrow Wilson International Center for Scholars, February 2007)

Morris, B., *Israel's Border Wars, 1949-1956: Arab Infiltration, Israeli Retaliation, and the Countdown to the Suez War* (Oxford: Oxford University Press, 1997) ISBN 0-19-829262-7

Nordeen, L., *Fighters Over Israel: The Story of the Israeli Air Force From the War of Independence to the Bekaa Valley* (London: Guild Publishing, 1991)

Nordeen, L., and Nicolle, D., *Phoenix over the Nile* (Washington: Smithsonian, 1996) ISBN 1-56098-826-3

Ovendale, R., *The Origins of the Arab-Israeli Wars* (Harlow: Longman Group UK Ltd, 1984) ISBN 0-582-49257-2

Riad, M., *The Struggle for Peace in the Middle East* (Consett: Quartet Books, 1981) ISBN: 978-0-704322-97-4

Safran, N., *From War to War: the Arab-Israeli Confrontation, 1948–1967* (New York: Pegasus Books, 1969) ISBN-13 978-0-672635-40-3

Shlaim, A., *The Iron Wall: Israel and the Arab World* (New York: W.W. Norton & Company, 2001) ISBN 0-14-028870-8

Stafrace, C., *Arab Air Forces* (Carrolton: Squadron/Signal Publications Inc., 1994) ISBN 0-89747-326-4

Tessler, M.A., *A History of the Israeli-Palestinian Conflict* (Bloomington and Indianapolis: Indiana University Press, 1994) ISBN-13 978-0253208736

Thompson, Sir R.E. (ed.), *War in Peace: An Analysis of Warfare since 1945* (London: Orbis Publishing, 1981) ISBN 0-85613-341-8

Thornhill, M., 'Britain, the United States and the Rise of an Egyptian Leader', *English Historical Review*, Volume CXIV, Issue 483 (September 2004), pp.893-94

Weiss, R., & Aloni, S., *Dassault Mystère IV* (Kefar-Tavor: IsraDecal Publications, 2010) ISBN 978-965-7220-13-9

Williams, A.G., & Gustin, Dr. E., *Flying Guns: the Modern* Era (Ramsbury: The Crowood Press Ltd, 2004) ISBN 1-86126-655-3

Zidek, P., 'Vyvoz zbrani z Ceskoslovenska do zemi tretiho sveta, 19481962', *Historie a vojenstvi*, 3/2002

Zidek, P., & Sieber, K., *Czechoslovakia in Middle East of the Years 19481989* (in Czech) (Prague: Ustav mezinarodnich vztahu, 2009) ISBN 978-80-86506-76-0

Various volumes of *Armed Forces Magazine*, published by the Egyptian Ministry of Defence, 1950s and 1960s; *El-Djeich* (official publication of the Algerian Ministry of Defence), various volumes from 2007 to 2009; various magazines and journals published by the Iraqi Air Force and the Iraqi Ministry of Defence, 1970s, 1980s and 1990s; *Kanatlar* magazine (Turkey), June 2003

Interviews with various Algerian, Egyptian, Iraqi and Syrian Air Force officers, pilots and ground personnel (see Acknowledgments and Endnotes)

ABOUT THIS BOOK

Sixty years after the tripartite aggression of France, Great Britain and Israel against Egypt, this is the first account specifically focussing on Egyptian military operations during the Suez War of 1956 (or 'Suez Crisis', as it is known in the West). Based upon research with help from official Egyptian documentation and the recollections of crucial participants, it provides a unique and exclusive insight into the 'other side' of a war that many consider marked 'the end of the British Empire'.

From the Western point of view, the situation is usually explained in quite simple terms: in retaliation for President Gamal Abdel Nasser's nationalisation of the Universal Suez Canal Company, and thus the strategically important waterway of the Suez Canal, France and Great Britan, operating in concert with Israel, launched an operation codenamed Musketeer. Divided into three phases, each shading into the other, this aimed to obliterate the Egyptian Air Force, occupy the entire Suez Canal and topple Nasser's government.

From the Egyptian point of view, the backgrounds were much more complex. Striving to modernise the country, a new and inexperienced government in Cairo launched a number of major projects, including one for the construction of a gigantic Aswan High Dam on the Nile. The only Western power ready to help finance this project, the USA, conditioned its support upon Egypt's provision of basing rights for the American military. With the last British soldiers still about to leave the country and thus supposedly ending Egypt's 'occupation by foreign powers for the first time in 2,000 years', Nasser found this unacceptable. Around the same time, Egypt found itself under pressure from Israeli raids against border posts on the Sinai peninsula. Left without a solution, Cairo decided to nationalise the Suez Canal in order to finance the Aswan High Dam project, but also to start purchasing arms from the Soviet Union. In an attempt to bolster Egyptian defences without antagonising Western powers, Nasser concluded the so-called 'Czech Arms Deal' with Moscow, resulting in the acquisition of Soviet arms via Czechoslovakia. Little realised in Cairo at the time, such moves tripped several 'red lines' – in Israel, and in the West, in turn prompting aggression that culminated in war.

Wings Over Sinai is primarily an account of the battle for survival of the Egyptian Air Force (EAF). Caught in the middle of conversion to Soviet-types, this force proved a match for Israel, although hopelessly ill-prepared to face the military might of Great Britain and France combined. Sustained, days-long air strikes on Egyptian air bases caused heavy damage, but nowhere near inflicting as crippling losses as was usually claimed and assessed by British, French and Israeli commentators. The EAF not only survived that conflict in quite good order, but also quickly recovered. This story is told against the backdrop of the fighting on the ground and the air and naval invasion by British and French forces.

Richly illustrated with plenty of new and often previously unpublished photographs, maps and 15 colour profiles, this action-packed volume illustrates all aspects of the camouflage, markings and various equipment of aircraft of both British and Soviet origin in Egyptian military service in 1956.

DAVID NICOLLE

David Nicolle, PhD, was born in London in 1944. He worked for BBC Television News and the BBC Arabic Service while also writing for educational magazines on various historical subjects, including aviation, before receiving a PhD from Edinburgh University. While continuing to write and illustrate articles for educational magazines, Dr Nicolle also started writing books on various aspects of aviation and military history, largely focusing upon the Arab and Islamic world. In 1983, he became a lecturer at Yarmouk University in Jordan, where he continued to teach until 1987. After returning to England, Dr Nicolle continued to write and now has over 100 books to his name, and has appeared in several TV documentaries.

TOM COOPER

Tom Cooper is an Austrian aerial warfare analyst and historian. Following a career in worldwide transportation business – during which he established a network of contacts in the Middle East and Africa – he moved into narrow-focus analysis and writing on small, little-known air forces and conflicts, about which he has collected extensive archives. That resulted in specialisation in such Middle Eastern air forces as those of Egypt, Iran, Iraq and Syria, plus various African and Asian air forces. As well as authoring and co-authoring 30 other books and over 500 articles, he has co-authored an in-depth analysis of major Arab air forces at war with Israel in the period 19551973, resulting in the six-volume book series *Arab MiGs*.

AIR VICE MARSHAL GABR ALI GABR

The late Air Vice Marshal Gabr Ali Gabr, PhD (EAF), served as a pilot in a De Havilland Vampire fighter jet during the Suez War of 1956. After concluding his higher military education at the Air Warfare Institute in 1960, he served as Instructor in Air Tactics at the Air Warfare Institute from 1962–1964 and 1966–1967, as Staff Officer during the June 1967 War, Chief of Operational Training Branch in the period 1968–1973 and as Chief of Operations Group during the October 1973 War with Israel. After serving as Instructor in the Art of Operations and Chief of the Air Force, the Chair at High War College from 1977 until 1982, and receiving his PhD at the Nasser High Academy in 1989, he moved into writing and published seven books and dozens of studies and articles on the history of air warfare in Egypt and abroad.

NOTES

Chapter 1

1 Thompson *et al*, pp.90-91
2 *Department of State Bulletin*, Vol. 22, p.886
3 Ovendale, p.137
4 Fullick & Powell, p.2
5 *Ibid*, p.137
6 Cull *et al*, p.20
7 Laron, p.17
8 Nasser, *The Philosophy of the Revolution*, Smith, Keynes & Marshall, 1955
9 Aburish, p.56, & Brown, p.159
10 Ovendale, p.138
11 Aburish, p.56, & Brown, p.159
12 Neff, p.43
13 Neff, p.177. The principal reason for Nasser's courting of the CIA before the Egyptian Revolution was his hope that the USA would act as a restraining influence on the British should London decide to launch a military intervention to end the revolution; see Thornhill, 'Britain, the United States and the Rise of an Egyptian Leader', *English Historical Review*, Volume CXIV, Issue 483 (Sept. 2004), pp.893-94.
14 Burns, p.11
15 Gaddis, p.168
16 Neff, p.177
17 Eveland, pp.84-90
18 Thompson *et al*, pp.90-91
19 Fullick & Powell, p.7
20 Fullick & Powell, p.7; Ovendale, p.139; Duff, p.136
21 Thompson *et al*, pp.132-133
22 Fullick & Powell, pp.68; Thompson, pp.75-78, 121-140
23 Aburish, p.56; Brown, p.159; Thompson, pp.121-140
24 Green, p.80
25 Ovendale, p.130
26 Green, pp.75-83
27 Green, p.99; Fullick & Powell, p.5
28 According to usual sources of reference, for example Martin Gilbert's *The Routledge Atlas of the Arab-Israeli Conflict* (ISBN 0-415-35901-5), no fewer than 967 Israelis were killed in 'Arab terrorist attacks' between 1951 and 1955. In comparison, Benny Morris declared such figures as 'pure nonsense' and 'based on a 1956 speech by David Ben-Gurion in which he used a phrase for casualties in their broad sense' (i.e. regardless if dead or wounded), and concluded that such figures were 'three to five times higher than the figures given in contemporary Israeli reports'; see Morris, p.101.
29 Orna Almog, *Britain, Israel, and the United States, 1955-1958: Beyond Suez*, p20. Almog cited Yeshoshfat Harkabi, former head of Israeli military intelligence, who stated that, 'these early infiltrations were limited incursions, motivated by economic reasons, such as Palestinians crossing the border into Israel to harvest crops in their former villages'. Furthermore, Shlaim, pp.84-85, writes: 'There is strong evidence from Arab, British, American, UN and even Israeli sources to suggest that for the first six years after the [1948] war, the Arab governments were opposed to infiltration and tried to curb it. The Lebanese ... effectively sealed the border with Israel. The Syrian authorities also exercised strict control over their border with Israel, and infiltration was rarer. The Egyptian authorities ... pursued a consistent policy of curbing infiltration until 1955 ... Secret Jordanian documents captured by the Israeli army during the June 1967 war ... reveal strenuous efforts on the part of the Jordanian military and civilian authorities ... to keep [infiltrators] from crossing [the Israeli border].'

Further evidence contrary to usual Israeli insinuations about infiltrations being 'sponsored, inspired, guided, or at least utilised' by Arab governments, was provided by Benny Morris, who cited an Israeli Foreign Ministry official in *Israel's Border Wars*, p.67:

'[W]hen (we) asked (the IDF for) ... some clear documentary proof of the (Arab) Legion's complicity (in the infiltrations) ... no clear answer came from the army. Finally, Fati (Deputy Minister of Internal Affairs, Yehoshafat Harkabi) told Leon (Savir, senior Foreign Ministry official) and myself, on two separate occasions, that no proof could be given because no proof existed. Furthermore, Fati told me that having personally made a detail study of infiltrations, he had arrived at the conclusion that Jordanians and especially the Legion were doing their best to prevent infiltrations, which was a natural decentralised and sporadic movement. In fact, listening to Fati or his colleagues these days, one could almost mistake them for British Foreign Office (which consistently argued in this vein).'

30 Green, p.99, & Shlaim, pp.128-129. The latter stressed: 'Records show that until the Gaza raid, the Egyptian military authorities had a consistent and firm policy of curbing infiltration ... into Israel ... and that it was only following the raid that a new policy was put in place, that of organising the fedayeen units and turning them into an official instrument of warfare against Israel.'
31 Green, p.99, & Neff, pp.54-55
32 Ovendale, p.133, & Shlaim, *Conflicting Approaches to Israel's Relations with the Arabs: Ben Gurion and Sharett, 1953-1956* (Washington, DC: International Security Studies Program, Woodrow Wilson International Center for Scholars, Smithsonian Institution, 1981), pp.131-4.

Chapter 2

1 While such conclusions might appear harsh, based on prejudice and even discrimination, readers might want to pay attention to the fact that a corresponding critique was repeatedly expressed by Gamal Abdel Nasser in his book *The Philosophy of the Revolution*.
2 Laron, p.7
3 Laron, p.8
4 The factory in question was virtually complete in 1951, when the Egyptians felt forced to dismiss the British personnel who were working there. When Egypt gave up hope of establishing reliable relations with Britain in early 1955, all the assembly jigs were sold back to Great Britain. What is notable is that domestic manufacture of aircraft was nothing new in Egypt. It originated as early as the 1920s and 1930s, when some domestically designed aircraft were developed and flown. However, it was only in 1955 that it launched series production of aircraft and even later that the local industry began providing services to the air force.
5 Green, p.114
6 Laron, pp.5, 8, 10-11, 13. Between the 1940s and 1980s, Czechoslovakia was one of the largest sellers of arms world-wide. Back in 1948, it was mainly Czechoslovakian weaponry – including fighter aircraft – which enabled Israel to conquer most of Palestine and defeat the armies of five neighbouring Arab states. What is less known is that Czechoslovakia also subsequently began selling arms to the Arabs.
7 Laron, pp.58, 16-17, 20-21
8 Cull *et al*, *Wings over Suez*, p.82; Green, p.121; Fullick & Powell, p.9; Laron, p.24. Notably, a smaller dam had been built by British engineers in 1898 four miles downstream from the position selected for the High Dam. Enlarged later on, it served the country well but was clearly for future agricultural expansion plans. The High Dam was designed to collect 26 times more water and increase the agricultural zone of Egypt by one sixth, making the nation self-sufficient in electrical power and mitigate the ever-present threat that some enemy might cut off Egypt's water by seizing control of the upper reaches of the Blue and White Niles.
9 Fullick & Powell, p.4
10 Green, p.121; Laron, pp.24-26. According to Laron, two additional factors supporting Nasser's decision appeared later during the year. The first was that after failing to find an agreement with Nasser, Eden sought an alternative base for British influence in the Middle East and found it in Iraqi Prime Minister Nuri as-Sa'id. The veteran politician, who bitterly resented the rejection of his 'Fertile Crescent' political federation scheme of the early 1940s in favour of the Arab League centred upon Cairo, and was eager to counter Nasser's claim to lead the Arab world, became instrumental in the establishment of the Middle East Treaty Organization (METO, also known as the 'Baghdad Pact'). Formed in February 1955, this included Iraq, Iran, Pakistan, Turkey and the United Kingdom and prompted Nasser to launch a propaganda campaign against the Iraqi and Jordanian governments, primarily via *Sawt al-Arab*.

The other fact appeared later in 1955, when anti-northern unrest erupted in southern Sudan. Because Nasser lacked the military capacity to launch a timely intervention, he was forced to abandon all pretentions to maintain control over Egypt's southern neighbour.

11 Pierre Pean, 'Les Deux Bombes', *Fayard* (Paris, 1982). Pean explains that the two nuclear programmes were closely intertwined and that while Israel lacked the necessary industrial infrastructure, the French learned a lot about technologies for developing and building nuclear weapons from Israeli nuclear scientists, many of these being US-born Jews who had participated in the Manhattan Project (the original US programme for development of nuclear weapons during the Second World War).

12 Weiss, p.4

13 Weiss, pp.67, & Cohen, p.89

Chapter 3

1 Cohen, pp.88-92

2 Hosni Mubarak joined the REAF as an officer cadet in February 1949. After graduating in March 1950, he spent two years in operational service. He returned to Bilbeis as an instructor in February 1952 and remained there for seven years. For most of the time, he served as an advanced flight instructor and flew Spitfires, but in 1957 he re-qualified for multi-engine aircraft and then specialised in bombers. This is why after the end of his service at the Air Force College, in January 1959, he was assigned the command of the EAF's sole bomber wing.

3 The number of Chipmunks acquired by Egypt from Canada might have increased to more than 50 by October 1956. Mustafa Abu Zaid was the younger brother of the famous Squadron Leader Mohammad Abu Zaid, the REAF's biggest hero of the Palestine War (who was killed in action in 1948). He learned to fly as a civilian and initially worked for Egyptian Airlines. He volunteered to serve as a bomber pilot in 1948, and subsequently flew Supermarine Sea Otter and Grumman Mallard amphibious planes. Mustafa Abu Zaid died in a non-flying related accident, while hunting ducks, in 1953.

4 David Nicolle, "Arabian Texans: T-6s, Harvards etc. with Middle East Air Arms', *Air Enthusiast* magazine, Volume 44/No. 97 (February 2002).

5 The FTU is believed to have been created through the merger of Nos 5 and 6 Squadrons, sometime in 1953. The reason for uncertainty is that from that period on, the exact identities of Egyptian squadrons have rarely been released officially.

6 Fuad Kamal, interview, February 1999; this and all subsequent information or quotations from Fuad Kamal are based on transcription of this interview and subsequent meetings.

7 Mustafa Shalabi el-Hinnawy, interview, March 1989; this and all subsequent information or quotations from Hinnawy are based on transcription of the same interview.

8 Letter by Dr Cattaneo of Aer Macchi to David Nicolle, & Foreign Office Memo, 18 November 1955 (PRO, Doc. 1955, FO 371, nos 113707, 113708, 113709, London). The total number of Vampires delivered to the EAF has never been officially released, but was clearly enough to equip at least two squadrons (Nos 30 and 31). According to Cattaneo, 43 of the Vampires in question were flown to Egypt (18 of these via Turkey and Syria in October 1955), while 15 were delivered in crates marked 'Fragile Murano Glass'. After considerable pressure from the British government, Italy admitted that 13 Vampires had been sold to Syria, 45 to another unidentified Middle Eastern country (obviously Egypt), and that 25 would soon go to Saudi Arabia.

9 The Meteor NF.Mk 13 was essentially a tropicalised version of the NF.Mk 11, equipped with larger intakes for its two Derwent 8 engines (necessary to help compensate for the ambient heat in the Middle East, which tended to reduce the thrust of early jet engines). Its radar, the AI.10, was essentially the British variant of the US-made SCR-720 set, developed during the Second World War for the Northrop P-61 Black Widow interceptor. The radar antenna of the AI.10 spun around through 360° on its vertical axis while at the same time slowly nodding between 50° up and 20° down to provide altitude coverage. The motor that drove the radar antenna was installed inside a small bump under the radome. The system was operated by the radar observer seated in the rear cockpit. It provided a c-shaped radar image of the airspace out to a range of about 22km (13½ miles) in front of the aircraft. Another characteristic of the Meteor NF.Mk 13 was its heavily framed canopy: this was not only an exceptionally heavy component, awkward to handle, but also one that restricted the view outside the cockpit.

Chapter 4

1 Wagdi Hafez (CO No. 7 Squadron in 1954-1956), interview with Nour Bardai, November 2015. Hafez used to serve with No. 2 Squadron, before being sent for an advanced course in Great Britain in 1954. Once back

home, he was assigned the command of No. 7 Squadron, which at that time operated 20 C-46s.

2 Gabr Ali Gabr's notes, & Laron, pp.27-28; Gabr's notes contain an observation about reports from British intelligence. Related to Mystère IVAs Israel ordered during the summer of 1955, this not only led to an assessment that such aircraft would provide Israel with air superiority throughout the Middle East, but also made the British worried about Israel planning an invasion of Jordan. This would have further strengthened Nasser's determination to purchase Soviet arms.

3 Zidek *et al*, & VUA-VHA, MNO, 1957, SMP, Karton 397, c.j. 001529-7/57-25-01, 4 November 1957, Czech National Archive. All the Soviet arms deliveries to Egypt were based on a commercial deal, not as some sort of aid, as is often suggested in the West. Therefore, Egypt had to pay for all the aircraft and other equipment it acquired, and there was nothing like an endless supply of these.

4 *Memorandum of Conversation at the White House*, from John Foster Dulles, 11 January 1956, Papers of John Foster Dulles, Box 10, Dwight D. Eisenhower Library.

5 Morris, p.291

6 Originally, Czechoslovakian MiG-15s wore the designation S.102: the MiG-15bis was S.103, and the MiG-15UTI CS.102. However, such designations were dropped in September 1956, while the Egyptians never made any distinctions between Czechoslovak- and Soviet-built aircraft, and therefore all aircraft delivered were regarded as MiG-15bis and MiG-15UTI.

7 Zidek *et al*, & VUA-VHA, MNO, 1957, SMP, Karton 397, c.j. 001529-7/57-25-01, 4 November 1957, Czech National Archive

8 Cooper *et al*, *Arab MiGs, Volume 1*, p.24; while some of No. 1 Squadron's pilots had earlier experience on Meteors and Vampires, most had previously flown piston-engined Hawker Furies.

9 For details on numbers of available Egyptian and Israeli pilots, see the following chapter.

10 Cull *et al*, p.86. According to Israeli sources, one of the MiG-15s involved in the first public appearance of the type in Egypt crashed while returning to base; see Even, p.6.

11 Zidek *et al*, & VUA-VHA, MNO, 1957, SMP, Karton 397, c.j. 001529-7/57-25-01, 4 November 1957, Czech National Archive; based on details provided in that document which summarises Operation 105, currently it is impossible to confirm reports about an order for 12 additional Il-28s, 100 MiG-17Fs, 40 Yak-11s and 18 different helicopters supposedly issued around the same time.

12 Zidek *et al*, & VUA-VHA, MNO, 1957, SMP, Karton 397, c.j. 001529-7/57-25-01, 4 November 1957, Czech National Archive

13 Labib, *The Third Arm*; this and all subsequent quotations from Labib are based on translations of excerpts from his book.

14 As far as is known, the highest attrition rate was experienced not during conversions to MiG-15, but by novice pilots learning to fly mechanically unreliable and sluggish Yak-11s, deliveries of which began only in August 1956. Three Yaks were written off in accidents that occurred before the Suez War; two were crashed while flown by instructors during rehearsal for a grand flypast to be reviewed by Nasser in September 1956. See Cull *et al*, p.98.

15 Even, p.9

16 Advertisement published in *The Armed Forces* magazine, April 1956. Obviously, the aircraft in question were MiG-15UTIs. Unsurprisingly, applicants were also advised not to eat breakfast prior to the flight.

17 *Memorandum for Admiral Arthur Radford* (Chairman, JCS), from Col George T. Powers, Plans and Operations Division, 27 February 1956, File 091 Palestine, Record Group 319, National Archives.

18 Even, p.5. In the course of Operation 104, Czechoslovakia (not France, as often reported) sold a number of German-made tanks (and their derivatives) of Second World War origin to Syria, including a total of 32 Sturmgeschütz III Ausführung Gs (StuGIII AusfG) 75mm self-propelled assault guns, 45 Panzerkampfwagen IVs (PzKpfwIV) and apparently a few Jagdpanzer IV/70s.

19 Gabr Ali Gabr's notes; interviews with Miroslav Irra and Josef Simon, 2012-2014.

20 Even, p.5. According to Israeli intelligence reports, training courses the Syrians received in the USSR were 'very intensive' and included night flying and flying in bad weather as well as air combat manoeuvring.

Chapter 5

1 Miroslav Irra, 'Drama na solnem jezere', *Letectvi & Kosmonautika*, 1999

2 Cull *et al*, p.63

3 Fullick & Powell, p.11

Duff, p.135

Fullick & Powell, p.13

Duff, p.137

Green, p.123

Duff, p.137

Gabr Ali Gabr's notes

0 Dayan, p.218. When requesting help from France, the Israelis claimed figures three times as high. Similarly, Cohen (p.105) listed Egypt as in possession of 210 aircraft, of which 150 were organised into 11 fighter and bomber squadrons, of which four operated MiG-15s and MiG-17s, three Vampires, one Meteors and two Il-28s.

1 Gabr Ali Gabr's notes; Ala'a Barakat, interview, March 2003; 'Air Superiority and Airfield Attack: Lessons from History', BDM Corporation Report, prepared for the Defense Nuclear Agency, 1982; 'Operation Kadesh, IDF/AF 1950–1956, Buildup and Operations', IDF/AF History Branch, 1986. Such high numbers of available Egyptian pilots might appear surprising to many, especially considering the never-ending flow of reports in the Western media about the EAF lacking qualified fliers and technical personnel, and reporting supposedly based on 'infallible Israeli intelligence'. However, they were confirmed by multiple additional sources, including statements by Nasser citing deployment of 250-260 pilots for conversion purposes to Czechoslovakia and Soviet Union in 1956, and documentation left behind by Abd el-Moneim el-Shennawy, who specified that after the Suez War he was sent to Czechoslovakia for a conversion course on MiG-15s together with 55 other pilots. The EAF could not have afforded sending so many pilots abroad for periods between three and 12 months if it was as short on pilots as so often reported.

2 VUA-VHA, MNO, 1957, SMP, Karton 397, c.j. 001529-7/57-25-01, 4 November 1957, Czech National Archive

3 Paul Gaujac, *Suez 1956* (Paris: Facon, 1986); VUA-VHA, MNO, 1957, SMP, Karton 397, c.j. 001529-7/57-25-01, 4 November 1957, Czech National Archive; & EAF Historical Department information via Sherif Sharmi.

14 Gabr Ali Gabr's notes, & EAF Historical Department information via Sherif Sharmi.

15 Eden, p.524; this and all quotations from Eden are excerpts from the same book.

16 Cull *et al*, *Wings over Suez*, pp.18788

17 Authors' personal notes, based on documents made available via the offices of the Armeé de l'Air Service Historique; for full text of this assessment, see Cull *et al*, pp.18788.

18 Based on cross-examination of information from Gabr Ali Gabr's notes, Ala'a Barakat, Labib, *The Third Arm* & information from the EAF Historical Department provided via Sherif Sharmi.

19 Even, p.2

20 Even, p.9

Chapter 6

1 Even, p.7, citing V.A. Zolotarev, *Russia in Local Wars and Military Conflicts in the Second Half of the 20th Century* (in Russian) (Moscow: Kuchkovo Pole, 2000), p.174. In the course of research for the book-series *Arab MiGs*, the authors were contacted by Argentinean researcher Diego Zampini, who travelled to Russia and interviewed a number of veterans of the Korean War. Some of them informed him that one of most important Soviet advisors in Egypt should have been Anatolievich Sintsov. Sintsov is known to have served with the 119th Interceptor Aviation Regiment (119. IAP) and flown Lavotchkin La-11 piston-engined fighters deployed in China, early in the Korean War. Subsequently, he converted to MiG-15s and helped train North Korean pilots on that type, but also flew some combat sorties. He was redeployed to Egypt in 1955, and is said to have been ordered to ferry two EAF MiG-17s out of the country on 3 November 1956, accompanied by an Egyptian pilot. Supposedly, once airborne, two MiG-pilots noticed a British aircraft just north of Port Said and decided to attack. Sintsov brought down a Wyvern fighter-bomber flown by Lieutenant Dennis McCarthy of 802 Naval Air Squadron of the Royal Navy (McCarthy ejected safely). Sadly, Sintsov passed away in 1990, shortly after barely mentioning his three claims from the Korean War in an article published in Russia, and without ever citing any kind of claims from the Suez War in public. Because of this, and because nobody else ever published any evidence in this regards, it remains unknown if he was really ever deployed to Egypt, or if he might have really downed McCarthy's Wyvern. All available Egyptian sources categorically deny even the possibility of any Soviet (or Czechoslovak) pilot flying combat sorties during the Suez War.

Nevertheless, similar reports were provided to researchers 'affiliated with the Institute for Military History of the Russian Federation's Ministry of Defence'. These claimed that 'Soviet flight instructors fought wing-by-wing with Egyptian pilots'. One of them reported: 'At dawn of 30 October, they managed (with MiG-15s) to intercept four English Canberra espionage planes and shoot down one. On the next day, 31 October, Soviet pilots took part in attacking the outposts of (IDF) Brigade 202. On 1 November, a group of MiG-17 interceptor planes from the USSR joined, especially for the battle, and on 2 and 3 November managed to shoot down several British fighter planes.' Other similar reports from Russian sources cited Soviet pilots flying Egyptian Il-28s and participating in 'uncharacteristic' combat operations. In one case (at an undetermined date), three Soviet-flown Il-28s encountered '10 British aircraft over the suburbs of Cairo' and, supposedly, 'two Hunters were shot down' by the Ilyushins.

Such legends are not only reserved for Russian sources. Doug Gordon wrote the following in the article 'USAFE's 38th TRS, 1952 to 1991', published in *AirEnthusiast* magazine, July/August 2007:

'On the fifth day of our rest (after the gruelling 40-minute flight from Brindisi to Larissa), we were taken to the Athens Int'l Airport, to be picked up by Maj Rufus Barnes (10th Tactical Recon Wing Ops) in [a Douglas] RB-26. While we were waiting to be picked up, standing in the shade of the US Naval Attache's [Grumman] SA-16, 21 MiG-15s landed and were refuelled by Royal Dutch Petroleum's fuel trucks (with white sidewall tires, no doubt bought with US dollars…). The Russian pilots were wearing flight suits without insignia or other markings. After refuelling, they took off, bound for Cairo. Over the Med, British and French pilots, flying NATO fighters based on Cyprus, intercepted the Russians. Nineteen MiGs were shot down en route, one was shot down on final approach to Cairo Airport, and the other MiG landed and was strafed on the taxiway. While that was happening, we were making the turn over Marseille, heading home, when we got a radio call to proceed directly to Spangdahlem [NATO air base in then West Germany], and go directly to 38th TRS operations. (At that time, we did not know about the shoot-downs: we found that out after landing at Spang). For three days, "the buzz" was that World War III was about to start. The Israeli Army had crossed the Suez, and was advancing towards Cairo. The Russian MiGs were supposed to assist the Egyptians, and counter the Israeli advance.'

Obviously, the 21 MiGs seen by the author while refuelling at Athens International might have been Syrian examples in the process of being evacuated via Greece instead of via Saudi Arabia, as usually reported. However, why anybody would risk flying them over the Mediterranean, the sky over which was full of Anglo-French aircraft in those days, remains beyond the comprehension of the authors.

2 Ex-Egyptian Vampires received serials F610-F616 in Jordanian service.

3 Cohen, p.105, & Cull *et al*, pp.99-100

4 Talaat Louca, interview, February 1999; this and all subsequent quotations from Talaat Louca are based on transcription of the same interview.

5 Interview and correspondence with Air Marshal Sa'ad ad-Din Sharif, acting ADC to President Sadat, 14 December 1973, Cairo (ad-Din Sherif had served in the RAF's No. 216 Transport and Ferry Group during the Second World War), & Ehud Yonay, *No Margin for Error: the Making of the Israeli Air Force* (New York: Pantheon, 1993), pp.16062.

6 According to Gabr Ali Gabr's notes, while considering the French-Israeli collaboration as possible especially in the light of the exposed position of Israeli paras at Mitla Nasser could not bring himself to believe that the British would get involved on the side of the Israelis.

7 The aircraft in question might have been an Avro Lincoln of the secretive No. 199 (Electronic Countermeasures) Squadron, RAF.

8 Abd el-Moneim et-Tawil, interview, February 1999; this and all subsequent quotations from Abd el-Moneim et-Tawil are based on transcription of the same interview.

9 Contrary to countless Israeli reports about Egyptians intending to deploy their Il-28s for attacks on population centres, no such orders were ever issued by the EAF, either during this war or any subsequent conflicts. All interviewed Egyptian Il-28 crews who either participated in operations against targets within Israeli proper, or heard about such operations, stress that their orders were explicitly related to military objects, primarily air bases.

10 After spending several months as a prisoner of war (POW) in Israel, Ahmad Faraghal returned to Egypt and continued his career with the EAF as a flight instructor. That was the rule for all the ex-POWs serving with EAF, and it was changed only after the June 1967 War, when there was a great need for fighter pilots.

11 Authors' notes, based on an article by A.B. Kotlobovkiy about Colonel A. Bozhenko's tour of duty in Egypt, in 1956-1957, published in the Ukrainian magazine *Aviyatsya & Vremya* in the 1990s; this and all

subsequent information or quotations from Bozhenko are based on translation of the same interview.

12 'The Wild Horses, the Mustang Squadrons', *Born in Battle* No. 44 (1987). Accordingly, a Mustang pilot 'K, forced down twice, by AA fire and an Egyptian Vampire, and thought dead, managed to hitch a ride back to Ekron and surprise his squadron commanders'. Cohen, pp.125-128, cites a loss under similar circumstances, on the same date and around the same time and place, but caused by ground fire.

13 Farouq el-Ghazzawi, interview, 1997; this and all subsequent quotations from Farouq el-Ghazzawi are based on transcription of the same interview.

14 To complete Fuad Kamal's story, here is part of his recollection detailing events following his landing by parachute:

'I landed badly and fell over backwards, hitting my head. Then I took off my parachute, collected it and buried it in the sand. I could still hear aircraft around. Then I was found by some bedouin but because I'm tall and rather fair, my family background is Circassian, they didn't believe I was an Egyptian. It took a long time to convince them. They cross-examined me and asked difficult questions, including about religion. Eventually, they seemed satisfied and took me to a tent, gave me a glass of milk and what looked like a small melon. They told me that el-Arish is a long way but I could go to an Egyptian heavy artillery battery at Bir Lahfan by foot, with two bedouin as guides.

'The air battle had been at around 13.30hrs in the afternoon and I arrived at Bir Lahfan around 22.00 at night. The position was surrounded by barbed wire and had guns in deep emplacements. I could only see a small light and hear a generator. Concerned about mines, I sat outside and waited. Eventually, I saw a soldier patrolling the other side of the wire and called out. He answered and I asked for an officer. They told me to stand up, with my hands raised. I could hear them cocking their guns. One soldier then came out to search me. He found my ID in my pocket. Then I was taken inside a bunker to be questioned. They asked military questions, addresses and so on, even what was on [at] the cinema the last week. An officer was sent to ask el-Arish about me. He was answered by an administrative officer who said there was no pilot with this name. So, I was asked more questions until one of the officers at el-Arish asked Air Vice Marshal Afifi about me. He replied, "You fool, don't you know about him?!?"

'After that they treated me well and I got dinner at Bir Lahfan. The place was called a "suicide post": they had been ordered not to retreat, so as to enable other units to withdraw. I was put in a truck straight to el-Arish, then to Qantara. We were shot at many times on the way and I could see the Canal Zone under attack. The officer in Qantara told me that Kabrit had been evacuated and my squadron had gone back to Cairo. So, I went to Cairo where most of [the] air force personnel was [sic] in civilian clothes and they thought I was dead.

'In Cairo, I called the Air Force Headquarters and was told to report to Abbasiya. There we assembled each day for orders. I didn't fly for the rest of the Suez War after that, but my squadron did fly a few missions from Almaza against the British in the Port Said area … Since surviving that ejection, I regard 31 October as my second birthday.'

Chapter 7

1 Barakat's recollection about a highly effective air strike on 202 Brigade was confirmed by several other sources, but most of these placed it at the Mitla Defile, although the Israeli column in question was attacked nearly 50km north-east of the strategic pass. For example, see Nordeen, p.43.

2 The French were not involved, as they did not have long-range bombers in service. Instead, their transport aircraft ferried supplies to Israeli units in Sinai.

3 Wagdi Hafez, interview with Nour Bardai, November 2015

4 Cull *et al*, *Wings over Suez*

5 Air Vice Marshal R.A. Mason & John W.R. Taylor, *Aircraft, Strategy and Operations of the Soviet Air Force* (London, 1986), p.65

6 Denis Albin, *Historique de l'Escadron de Chasse 1/3 Navarre de 1915 à 2000* (relevant excerpt forwarded by French reader of the *Arab MiGs* book-series). Sadly, more precise details about such claims are unlikely to become available as it is understood that all documentation relating to AdA operations from Israeli air bases during the Suez War has been destroyed in order to preserve the secrecy of this affair.

7 Even, p.5, based on Air Intelligence Report No. 28, 11 November 1956, Air Force HQ, Air Branch 4, MD/6/2143, IDFA, file 675-535/2004. According to Even, '23 Syrian planes were damaged' during the Suez War. This number might include three out of four MiG-15UTIs that were eventually evacuated to Syria via Saudi Arabia and Jordan, and 20 MiG-15bis from the

second batch ordered by Syria, that were not fully assembled and stored at Abu Suweir.

8 Cull *et al*, *Wings over Suez*, p.235.

9 This aircraft was donated to the SyAAF after the war.

10 Mohammad Nabil el-Masry, interview with Lon Nordeen, 1997; this and all subsequent quotations from Nabil el-Masry are based on transcription of the same interview.

11 Denis Albin, *Historique de l'Escadron de Chasse 1/3 Navarre de 1915 à 2000* (relevant excerpt forwarded by French reader of the *Arab MiGs* book-series).

12 Cull *et al*, pp.213, 231

13 Obviously not knowing about Nasser's order for the EAF to stop fighting, Air Marshal Denis Barnett, Air Task Force Commander of the RAF, stated that, 'if we had been up against an enemy with even a modicum of fighting qualities with the modern aircraft and equipment the Egyptians had, the situation would have been different' (see Cull *et al*, p.198).

14 Gabr Ali Gabr's notes

15 Rumours still circulating in Egypt that 'some' Vampires from Nos 2 and 31 Squadrons were redeployed at air bases on the Sinai peninsula cannot be confirmed.

16 Cull *et al*, p.237

17 Ibid, pp.250, 260

18 Ibid, pp.271, 277

19 Tahir Zaki, interview, February 1999; this and all subsequent information or quotations from Tahir Zaki are based on transcription of the same interview.

20 Morris, pp.419-425

21 'Royal Saudi Air Force Museum', *Aviation News*, September 2010. According to the article in question, Saudi Arabia purchased 19 Vampires from Egypt (including the example 1541, which is still on display at the Royal Saudi Air Force Museum wearing serial number 541). Considering 12 of these were delivered before 29 October, this would mean that at least seven Vampires survived the war.

22 Even, p.5, based on Air Intelligence Report No. 28, 11 November 1956, Air Force HQ, Air Branch 4, MD/6/2143, IDFA, file 675-535/2004. According to same report, '23 Syrian planes were damaged' during the Suez War. This number might include three out of four MiG-15UTIs that were eventually evacuated to Syria via Saudi Arabia and Jordan, and 20 MiG-15bis from the second batch ordered by Syria. The aircraft of this second batch appear not to have been delivered to Syria after the Suez War: on the contrary, the appearance of MiG-15bis with serial numbers in the range 901-999 in Egyptian service in the late 1950s indicates that all were either donated or sold to Egypt. The EAF never issued serial numbers in that range to its MiG-15bis (see Table 4 for details). According to Even, the third batch of combat aircraft ordered by Syria included 16 MiG-17s, which arrived in Egypt during November 1956.

23 Zidek *et al*, & VUA-VHA, MNO, 1957, SMP, Karton 397, c.j. 001529-7/57-25-01, 4 November 1957, Czech National Archive

24 For details on repeated Egyptian demands for delivery of napalm bombs from the USSR, see Cooper *et al*, *Arab MiGs Volume 3 & Volume 4*.

25 Cooper *et al*, *Arab MiGs Volume 3*, p.203

26 Williams *et al*, p.79

27 Ibid, p.79